THE
HOME INSPECTION
HANDBOOK

THE HOME INSPECTION HANDBOOK

Hugh Howard

for

Home Renovation Associates

DOUBLEDAY & COMPANY, INC.
GARDEN CITY, NEW YORK
1987

Illustrations by Doris Borowsky

Library of Congress Cataloging-in-Publication Data
The Home inspection handbook.

   1. Dwellings—Inspection. I. Home Renovation
Associates.
TH4817.5.H67 1987   643'.12   86-6205
ISBN 0-385-23194-6

ACKNOWLEDGMENTS

This book is the product of many years of experience on the part of a great variety of professionals. It is the result of the generosity of many people with their time and energy.

In alphabetical order, Home Renovation Associates acknowledges the help of: Richard Bennett, A.I.A., for his common-sense approach to thinking about the design and layout of houses; Lorentz Kafka, proprietor of Red Rock Real Estate, for his copious and invaluable commentary; David A. Thurm, Esq., whose thoughtful reactions suggest that though he is a lawyer by profession his heart may pine for the building trades; and Glenn D. Williams whose shingle reads "insurance," but behind whose easy grin is the heart and soul of an editor. Thanks, too, to others too numerous to mention—the plumbers and electricians and pipe fitters and millworkers and the rest who have answered with patience the hundreds of questions asked of them as this book was put together. And to John Gallagher, who helped transform an idea into a book.

To these gentlemen go thanks, but none of the blame; if anything in these pages misleads, the fault lies here and not with them.

Hugh Howard
General Editor
Home Renovation Associates

CONTENTS

INTRODUCTION

We all have heard horror stories about people who bought a home that they thought was a dream come true—only to discover that the house had expensive or dangerous problems. *The Home Inspection Handbook* is designed to help you avoid being the subject of just such a story.

Inevitably, after the first blush of enthusiasm, the buyer who is about to plunk down his or her life savings is wary. "What's wrong with it?" is nothing if not a logical question in that circumstance. The home buyer's primary concern, therefore, is to learn where and how to look for the symptoms that indicate existing or future problems. There will be some, rest assured of that; even those houses that the real estate ads term "immaculate" will have something wrong. It may be simply the absence of a good bolt lock on the back door, but you must anticipate that no house is perfect: as is true of people, there are aspects that will make you want to be its friend forever, others that will leave you wondering how true a friend it will be.

The purpose of this book is to teach you how to read the symptoms and make a comprehensive diagnosis of your prospective new home in a matter of hours, even without a thorough grounding in plumbing, basic construction, electricity, or the other building trades. This

book will tell you which of the problems you uncover require immediate attention, which of them are serious and
which are not. Armed with the information in *The Home
Inspection Handbook*, you can make informed judgments
about the condition of the house you are about to buy and
the maintenance problems you are likely to have.

WHAT KIND OF HOMEOWNER
WILL YOU BE?

The Home Inspection Handbook will help you approach your to-buy-or-not-to-buy decision from a variety
of angles. In order to consider the desirability of an extrav-
agantly detailed Victorian house, for example, you must
consider the practical implications of the gingerbread trim
and the enormous porch. They represent, in a word, up-
keep. Are you prepared to paint or reconstruct or tear
down the decorative extras that are so much more exposed
to the elements? Throughout this book, we will raise questions like this one for your consideration, and try to help
you answer them.

Identify yourself as one of three basic types of home
buyers: a Rookie, an Apprentice, or a Handyman. The
classic profile of a Rookie is a lifelong city dweller. He is
looking to move his wife and new baby from their rental
apartment downtown in a major metropolitan city to a
one-family house in a suburb. These homeowners-to-be
know virtually nothing about home ownership: he was
born to a family of apartment dwellers, has always lived in
an apartment, and thinks that it is the building superinten-
dent's job to fix things. Changing a light bulb may be
within the Rookie's ken, but he wouldn't know a pipe

wrench from a crescent wrench. His is a problem not only of inexperience but also of confidence.

At the other extreme is Mr. Handyman. When he was barely old enough to ride a two-wheeler he was taking it apart and, more surprisingly, putting it back together. He is a whiz with tools and his idea of fun is spending a weekend putting a new roof on a friend's summer camp. He is ready to take on whatever problems his new house offers and is prepared to move his two tons of tools into that spacious, two-bay garage tomorrow.

In between the Rookie and the Handyman is the Apprentice: he or she is game, helped Dad unclog the sink a few times, and probably has done a fair amount of painting and other superficial renovating of apartments or rented houses over the years. The Apprentice has a little tool sense, is willing to try to solve a problem when it has to be confronted, but given a choice would just as soon steer clear of household hassles.

Throughout this book the Rookie, the Apprentice, and the Handyman will make cameo appearances. The particular interests of each will be addressed (a kitchen that needs remodeling may present a desired challenge to a Handyman, but a Rookie may see it as an excellent reason to say no thank you to the real estate agent). Pick the category to which you and your skills and inclinations—or lack of them—belong. And put yourself and your house into perspective with the problems and solutions offered by the Rookies, Apprentices, and Handymen.

HOW TO USE THIS BOOK

Whether or not you buy a particular home is likely to come down to an instinctive, emotional decision. But you may find the inspection task easier if you try to assume the role of a detective, a sort of domestic investigator.

Your goal is to discover as much as you can about the house: its history, strengths, and weaknesses, the good news and the bad. Your method should be to follow every clue you come across in the process. No door should remain unopened, no corner uninvestigated.

Don't be distracted by furnishings, by rugs and pictures and people and noises. You can no more afford to be concerned with such factors than your doctor can with the color or quality or cut of your shirt or blouse—it's the skin and bones and organs that count, not what hides them.

Read this book before you inspect. If you try to read it as you conduct the inspection, you will find yourself taking more time than necessary and probably failing to see critical evidence. As you read, if you find building or technical terms you do not recognize, check them in the Glossary at the end of the book.

Your inspection should follow the organization of the book. The first of the three parts of the book concerns "The Exterior." You begin outside, at Checkpoints 1 through 5—The Yard and the Neighborhood, External Wall Coverings, Indoor/Outdoor Spaces, The Roof, and The Garage and Other Outbuildings.

Next are the internal structure and mechanisms of the house. In the unfinished areas, confirming evidence may be found to support suspicions raised by the external examination, or even to indicate future problems, problems that may be years away from maturing but that are inevitable unless immediate steps are taken. In Part II you will visit checkpoints concerning The Foundation, Termites and Other Insects, The Electrical System, Heating and Air Conditioning, Water, Plumbing, and Hot Water Heaters, The Attic, and Insulation.

Part III takes you into the living spaces of the home. The quality of the interior finish will be examined, along with the condition of the appliances, the utility of the layout, and the patterns of ventilation. The checkpoints include Fireplaces and Chimneys, Floors, Interior Walls and Ceilings, Windows and Doors, The Kitchen, The Bathroom, and Design and Layout.

THE CHECKSHEET: As you go from one checkpoint to the next, you may find it useful to have this book with you for reference, but it is the Checksheet that begins on page 207 that is to be your tour guide. Make photocopies of the Checksheet; take extra pages for miscellaneous notes and observations.

Make notes as you go; fill in the blanks of your Checksheet. As you will be trying to absorb a great deal in a short time, the notes and Checksheet will be valuable to you later in helping you recall all that you saw. Patterns in your observations may emerge that give you insight into the strengths or, more likely, the weaknesses of the house.

Follow-ups are all-important. Periodically in the text there are references to clues you may find at one checkpoint that have bearing on issues discussed in later checkpoints. Make sure you follow up the awkward dip in the roof you saw from outside when you are in the attic later on. A notation on your Checksheet will help you remember to do so.

We recommend at least two trips in and out and around the house. More are better still; it takes time to see through furnishings and preconceptions and habit. And we all kid ourselves a little bit—at first we don't see what we don't want to see, but sometimes a second and third look will reveal what we missed earlier.

THE IMMEDIATE
IMPROVEMENT INDEX

Most of the issues raised in this book are about small problems. If the lawn needs reseeding, that's not a big deal; a chip in the porcelain bathtub is hardly a health hazard. You will be asked literally hundreds of questions in these pages, most of which concern details of the house.

However, as you inspect you may uncover problems that are more than matters of taste or quality of material or normal wear and tear, concerns that not only need immediate attention but will cost you more than the price of a quart of paint or a few wood screws.

Enter the Immediate Improvement Index. At the close of each checkpoint and on the Checksheet, you will find a summary of the serious problems you may have found as you inspected. These serious problems will be rated: like burns, they come in three degrees. Since the costs of labor and materials vary widely, it is impossible to estimate accurately the cost of typical home improvements, but in general, the Immediate Improvement Index is as follows:

A rating of *I* means an investment of up to two hundred dollars is necessary. While the *I* reading on the Immediate Improvement Index means that the work must be done (no optional tasks are included on the Index; the intention is to warn you of problems that must be solved immediately), a *I* also means that little or no construction will be involved, and a willing Apprentice or Handyman can probably deal with the problem. An example of a reading of *I* is the need to replace a few broken panes of glass in the basement windows.

II suggests more serious trouble, but an investment of not more than a thousand dollars. A new hot water heater would rate a *II*: a hot water heater typically costs somewhere between two hundred and fifty and five hundred dollars to purchase and install. Other examples of a *II* might be a garage door that needs to be replaced or several very scratched and stained wood floors in the house that require sanding and refinishing.

III could cost thousands of dollars; *III* means substantial expert help and expensive materials are required. A new roof rates a *III*, as would the need to replace the furnace or rewire the entire house.

If you come across any problems in the house you're considering that are rated on the Immediate Improvement Index, note them prominently on your Checksheet. When it comes to making your final decision, these problems—perhaps a single one with a *III* rating or the sum of a number of lesser ones—may weigh heavily in your buying decision.

THE WALK-AWAY FACTOR

For every home buyer there is a point at which it is time to withdraw the offer, to forget about the house and start thinking about the next one. That point may be different for the skilled Handyman than for the Rookie, but when the foundation is crumbling, the pipes corroded, and a nuclear waste dump is found in an adjacent lot, well, it's time to walk away, no matter what your skills.

At the close of each chapter, any entries on the Immediate Improvement Index will be accompanied by a listing of those chronic problems (if any) that are in themselves arguments for trying another house. The fact is, any problem can be fixed—but at what cost? You can move a house away from Love Canal, but the price may be many tens of thousands of dollars. You can reconstruct a foundation, you can replumb, you can throw money at virtually any problem. But when the trouble is so serious as to deserve the label "Walk-Away Factor," make sure you think thrice before buying.

WHEN TO INSPECT

You should conduct your inspection before contract if possible. If it isn't, get your lawyer to negotiate a clause into the contract making it subject to a thorough inspection.

If the house is not lived in, ask the seller to arrange for the utilities to be turned on. You will want to test appliances, look into dark closets, and perform a variety of examinations made possible (or easier) by the presence of electricity or gas.

If you cannot conduct certain tests because you were unable to arrange for the power to be on, get the seller to represent on paper that everything works. If the water is off, get the same written assurance about the water supply and the size of the sewage system. Then you have grounds for going back to him if problems arise.

Conduct your inspection during the day; no matter how bright artificial illumination is, you will see more in natural light.

TOOLS AND DRESS

You need only a few common tools you probably already own, including a tape measure, a hammer, a jackknife, a screwdriver, and a flashlight. A pair of binoculars is helpful for inspecting the roof. You should also buy an inexpensive electrical tester at your local hardware store (the simplest one, available for two or three dollars, will do nicely).

Clothes? The older the better, preferably long-sleeved and sturdy, but not confining, as basements and attics are dirty, with awkward corners.

IS IT THE RIGHT HOUSE FOR YOU?

In a sense, the goal of this book is to help you answer three basic questions: First, can you live in the house? Second, is the house well made—that is, how good were the materials and how well were they used? Third, are the problems you found curable within the limitations of your budget and your skills as a Handyman, Apprentice, or Rookie?

This book is not intended to be a substitute for a professional inspector. On the contrary, in a nation where the average house price is approximately a hundred thousand dollars, the investment of a few hundred dollars for a professional inspection may make sense to you, even after you have made your inspection; if you've looked first, then you can direct an inspector to areas of concern and be sure he is doing his job well.

As you inspect the house, you should also keep in mind that as you discover problems, be they serious or minor, citing them specifically may put you in a better negotiating position, assuming you have not established all the terms of the sale. After all, if you are going to have to spend money making the place safer or more suitable to your needs, then perhaps that can be used to negotiate a lower price, or to change other terms in the agreement.

This book should help you focus your attention on practical things. It should help you get a sense today of what you are in for tomorrow. While you can actually inspect only the visible portions of the house's systems, you can get a valid overall reading of the house's health. An experienced professional will be the first to warn you that the newest, best-designed, and most carefully maintained piece of equipment can break down suddenly, without prior warning, but that same electrician or steamfitter or plumber will also tell you that most of the time the clues are there to be picked up in advance.

Follow the directions given in each of the nineteen checkpoints. Use the Checksheet, filling in the blanks and entering your comments. Record each and every problem that rates a mention on the Immediate Improvement Index and keep a careful eye out for Walk-Away Factors. When you finish, review the assessment procedures in the closing chapter of the book. We can't tell you whether to buy the house or not, but after your inspection you should be armed with enough information to decide for yourself.

So good luck and good hunting—and may the best house win your love, happiness, and mortgage account.

Part I

THE EXTERIOR

THE YARD AND
THE NEIGHBORHOOD

Bill and Beverly Friedman moved into their new house upon returning from their honeymoon. To them, the pristine colonial on the Connecticut coast was perfect: set up onto a little hillock, it overlooked Long Island Sound, with a grand view reminiscent of the grander age in which the house was built.

Their first month there was equally perfect. But then spring came, and the ground thawed. Overnight, their front lawn turned into a swamp. They soon discovered that not only was it a marshland nine months of the year, but that given state statutes about preserving wetlands, there was nothing they could do.

When investing in real estate, such concerns as the size of a piece of property and the real estate values in a given neighborhood are very important indeed. However, the primary purpose of this book is not to guide you as an investor, but to help you to determine whether the house you want to buy is safe and well constructed, and that things are as appealing as they seem. We can't promise that by inspecting your home you can be assured the purchase price is right, but we are trying to help you avoid painful morning-after discoveries like Bill and Beverly's.

The best way to begin the inspection is with a survey map of the property. Ask the seller if the property has been surveyed. Many banks require a survey before granting a mortgage, so the odds are that one exists if the house has changed hands in recent years.

Walk the boundaries of the property with the survey in hand. It's best if you use a photocopy, as you may want to make marks and jot down questions on the document for later discussion with the seller.

Do the property lines coincide with those you were led to believe were the real ones on your first look? There are many instances where sellers have made significant changes in property lines, particularly when they are holding onto adjacent properties. In one instance we know of, a turn-of-the-century estate was being subdivided on New York's Long Island, and a spectacular row of lilacs and other flowering bushes suddenly disappeared from the acreage assigned to one of the houses. A squiggly line was all that remained on the survey, neatly reassigning the lilacs to the property the seller was retaining. Fortunately the buyers were alert and noticed the change before the closing, and insisted that the gardens be reincorporated into their property.

Are there any right-of-ways or other interferences that may be indicated from adjacent pieces of property? Even if none is indicated on the survey, be sure your lawyer checks your deed. In one case we know of in a suburb of Boston, a homeowner woke up one morning to find bulldozers transforming his strawberry patch into a streetbed. The previous owner had granted a right-of-way to a local developer, and, years later, the developer took advantage of his option and constructed an access road as the deed allowed him to do. His next step was the construction of several dozen houses on the land he owned—land that was virtually in our friend's backyard!

It is also an excellent idea to know what the zoning is in the area of the house. The zoning may work either to your advantage or disadvantage, but you should know. Will it allow you to make the renovations you want (Thinking about putting an apartment in over the garage to rent out? The zoning may prohibit it); what can your neighbors do that would affect you (How would you feel about a filling station next door if you are in or adjacent to a commercial zone?)? A trip to City Hall to consult the zoning map will quickly and easily reassure you on these points.

Look at the house from the extremes of the property; look at the views of other homes and buildings nearby. Do you see anything that makes your eyes sore? An ugly house across the street, an abandoned VW underneath a neighbor's tree, even an unkept lawn next door can make your attempts to keep your house and yard beautiful seem more than a little futile.

LAWNS AND LANDSCAPING . . . AND DRAINAGE

Is the grass or other ground cover healthy, or are there brown or bare spots? Does it appear to have been carefully mowed and raked? Is the yard level? If not, must it be leveled for your purposes, or will it require special maintenance (for example, mowing a thirty-degree slope is dangerous with a power mower)? Are there areas where the soil has eroded from water runoff? If so, the dirt will look like a dry streambed, with gullies visible between the stones and rocks that remain.

In fact, the drainage of water should, except in very arid parts of the country, be your single most important consideration at this checkpoint. It is an issue both within your yard and without, and eroded soil is one of the key clues to understanding the drainage patterns on the property.

The more developed the area, the more likely it is that the runoff will be a problem. When houses are separated by a good deal of undeveloped land, nature makes its own ways, and with a minimum of man's intervention rain and meltwater can be directed to paths away from houses. But when every square inch of surface is covered with lawns and driveways and tennis courts, culverts and storm drains must do the work that natural streambeds did.

Locate yourself with respect to the topography of your surroundings. If you are at or near the top of a hill, you probably will not be subject to water pooling in your yard or basement, so you should be most concerned with simple soil erosion. This can be dealt with by planting grass or other vegetation on the slope to limit it. (However, if there is growth already and there is still an erosion problem, you may have to resort to a retaining wall. See the discussion of retaining walls, page 11.)

If you are on a slope or at the bottom of one or if there is a stream or swamp near the level of the yard, you must be especially conscious of the runoff patterns around your house. Even if it rains only once a year, if the water falls from the sky and is directed by a sloping yard toward the house, you'll have a problem, probably in your basement and foundation.

As you walk around the house, make sure the property slopes away from it at the rate of at least one inch per foot, for a distance of at least ten feet. To judge this, stand about twenty feet from the house and eyeball the slope— the exact pitch doesn't matter, just be sure there is a noticeable slope away from your foundation.

While a little soil erosion on a bank on the far side of the yard is only a matter of appearances and can generally be solved with a few yards of soil and a bag of seed, water that runs into the basement frequently may endanger the very structure of the house. Gullies beneath the eaves, puddles or other signs of water moving toward the house and foundation should be noted on your Checksheet and followed up at Checkpoint 6, where we will help you determine the severity of the problem.

Keep an eye out for pipes that emerge from the foundation, too; note them on your Checksheet for follow-up in the next checkpoint, as they may well be part of a sump pump or other pumping system.

TREES, SHRUBS, AND GARDENS

Are the trees healthy, or do the leaves show signs of extensive insect damage and the limbs appear dead and leafless? Do any of the trees or their limbs extend over the house or interfere with the telephone or electrical wiring? Are any of the trees very large and beginning to look as if they might require removal or serious surgery?

Serious tree problems are those that require hiring a tree surgeon (the work can be dangerous and the inexperienced Apprentice and Rookie would do well to avoid climbing trees wielding chain saws). An occasional dead limb on a pine tree is to be expected; a giant tree with several dead limbs, one of which is about to fall on the house, means professional help is required. A tree surgeon can do remarkable things to even the biggest trees with guide wires and cement, but such work is by no means inexpensive. Are there signs of soil erosion at the foot of any of the trees? If many large roots are visible, the tree may be unstable and could be a very serious hazard in a gale-force wind.

Consider what time of year it is. If you are inspecting when the foliage is full, determine which of the trees are deciduous and try to imagine what effect the absence of the leaves will have on the privacy of your backyard (deciduous trees are those with leaves that fall rather than needles like the evergreens). Do the trees or shrubs act as a barrier between you and the road or a neighbor's yard that essentially disappears when the leaves fall?

Are there any roots that protrude that could be dangerous, threatening to trip a guest taking a walk after dinner? Any large trees in the immediate vicinity of the house or sewage system may also present problems, as the roots can be enormously strong and may cause cracking or heaving in a driveway, cellar, or other subterranean concrete structure. If there are very substantial trees immediately adjacent to the house, note that fact on your Checksheet for follow-up at Checkpoint 6 where we will inspect the foundation for cracking and other problems.

Do you like the appearance of the trees? Is there a satisfactory balance of shady and sunny spots? Trees can be planted, of course, but even a fast-growing softwood requires a number of years of growth before it can provide any significant shade.

As for the shrubs, bush plants, or hedgerows, are there any that are brown or lifeless? Have they been properly cared for? A neat, trimmed shape is often the best indication of this. If you are not familiar with any of the varieties present, make a note to ask the seller if any of them require special care: some bushes in colder climates will need coverings to protect them from the weight of the snow, for example, while others may require extra watering during the warmer months.

Many people take great pleasure and pride in caring for plants, but you must decide whether or not you want to take on the task. This is particularly true with elaborate gardens. A beautiful garden is a source of great pleasure to some people but requires care and feeding to get the same result every year. Handymen aren't necessarily gardeners, but the same work ethic applies here. If you are a Rookie gardener and have zero desire to learn, think twice about the house with the terraced plantings of annuals and perennials, with the trained vines and shrubs that must be pruned. Otherwise, the garden questions are essentially the same as those of the tree and bush cover: What is there, do you like it, and what condition is it in?

If the sort of garden you want to have is not there, is there room for it? And are the conditions suitable? Sunlight and soil must be your first considerations, but think also about a source of water and storage space for the tools and other paraphernalia.

FENCES, RETAINING WALLS, AND OTHER CONSTRUCTIONS

If there are any fences, stone or brick walls, or other manmade partitions on the property, are they in good condition? Look for missing pieces, peeling paint, and any signs of advanced deterioration like bent or broken members. If there is a gate, open and close it to be sure it is in good working condition.

If there are wooden fences, it is their lowermost portions that you should be concerned with, as soil level is where you are most likely to encounter decay. Decayed wood is commonly referred to as "dry rot." In fact, dry rot isn't dry at all; it would be more accurate to call it "wet rot" or "damp rot"—a piece of wood that was always dry would never rot. Dry rot occurs when wood is alternately wet and dry; wood that is submerged in water, like a pier, is much less likely to sustain rot damage than wood in, say, a fence post that is subject to wetness whenever it rains but is dry the rest of the time.

To test for decayed wood, hold your screwdriver in your fist and jab it into the wood at ground level. The force required is more than a tap but less than a punch. If the blade makes more than a slight indentation, there is some softening of the wood due to dry rot. Make a number of test probes to determine the extent of the softness. If the screwdriver penetrates the wood easily and deeply, serious rot is present, and replacement of the posts necessary.

Fixing fences is a task an Apprentice might well be able to take on, although digging postholes, carting heavy timbers, and sawing can be challenging work.

Test the strength of the fence from up high as well as at ground level. If children or adults are likely to try to sit or climb on them, you surely don't want your fences dangerously close to collapsing.

When it comes to stone walls, more often the tops present problems. Don't walk on the wall (this is a good way to sprain an ankle or take a hard fall), but determine if the top stones are loose or wobbly. A good mason will have used the largest, flattest stones on top for stability and to keep water out of the wall—check to see if that is the case. Is there moss or lichen growing on the wall that could cause a climbing child to slip and fall? (If you have a bad back, don't try to take on stone wall repair yourself.)

If the fencing is metal, is it rusted? Is it solidly footed

in concrete, or does the metal disappear directly into the soil? If so, it will probably rust away in a few years. Is the material unsightly or dangerous (many a converted farm property will have rusted barbed wire hidden in the old leaves at the edge of onetime pastures).

If any of your property has a steep slope, a retaining wall may be needed to contain soil that otherwise will gradually erode down the slope. If a wall is there, make sure it is solid (if the house is north of the frost line and the ground is still frozen at the time of your inspection, don't be deceived; what's rigid in January may be dangerously loose in April's rains). Look for missing pieces, for cracks if it is concrete, or other general signs of wear and tear. Check the pitch of the wall, too. It should lean into the hill; if it leans forward, there will probably be trouble in the next year or two.

DRIVEWAY, SIDEWALKS, AND UTILITY SURFACES

Are the outside surfaces in good repair? Look for cracks in asphalt, concrete, or masonry surfaces. Have any portions eroded away? Look at the edges of the driveway in particular for signs of soil erosion. Bad drainage is more often the cause of driveway problems than anything else. Even a Rookie—with the desire—can take on a small landscaping project, but keep in mind that moving soil and crushed stone is hard, blister-inducing labor.

Is the surface flat, or will your car bottom scrape at the mouth of the driveway where it intersects the road? If the driveway opens onto a well-traveled street, can you see the traffic coming from both directions as you pull out? Check the pitch of the driveway: Does it run toward the house and will it direct water into the foundation or lower levels of the house? If so, mark your Checksheet for follow-up at Checkpoint 5 or Checkpoint 6.

How long is the driveway? If you live in a part of the country where snowfall is considerable, you may find shoveling that long drive a great deal of work.

Is there enough room in the driveway for your car(s)? This is particularly important if the town or city limits parking at night or during inclement weather. Is it wide enough? It is recommended that your driveway be at least eight feet wide, and ten feet is a minimum if the primary route of entry for pedestrians is also the driveway.

If there is a sidewalk that runs parallel to the street, determine if it is municipally maintained. Often the town or city owns the sidewalks but leaves maintenance to the homeowner. Ask at City Hall. Are there potholes or heaves in your walkways that endanger pedestrians? Are there any other signs of uneven settling like cracks or patches? These sorts of problems can be dealt with by an Apprentice with relatively inexpensive materials available from most building material stores.

Are there any steps or abrupt changes in level of the walks? If there are three or more steps, there should be a handrail; with only one or two, no railing is necessary. Some kind of landmark, like a shrub, should point out to the visitor unfamiliar with the terrain that there is a change in level.

Is the patio level, or will your umbrella table stagger off the edge, and your food end up in your lap? A slant toward the foundation of the house can be troublesome on another count as well, since it may direct water into the foundation or basement.

Is the surface of the patio broken by cracks or heaves that may trip your guests? Cracks in concrete can be patched easily, but many wide cracks (more than a quarter inch wide) usually indicate that patching is only a temporary solution, and that its foundation is inadequate, causing it to settle unevenly and crack. Unless the settling is so extreme that the patio becomes tricky to walk on, the concern is more one of appearance (cracks are unsightly) than of safety.

If the patio surface is wood, it should be made of lumber that was pressure-treated to resist decay. When new, pressure-treated lumber is a sickly green color that fades as it weathers. It can be left in contact with soil (though this is not recommended) but no other wood should be. Patios and decks (see Checkpoint 3) have a greater life expectancy if made of pressure-treated lumber than if the wood used was untreated or merely dipped or coated with a preservative unless they are painted every other year. Check the wood surface for softness and decay. (If the house has an attached deck or porch, see Checkpoint 3.)

OTHER CONCERNS

Is there a bin or other location for your garbage? You may find that the neighbors's dogs play havoc with the garbage after dark if it isn't secure.

Is there adequate outdoor lighting? If you want to barbecue and eat on that picnic table out back, will you be doing so by candlelight? Is there an outdoor electrical outlet near the outdoor living space for plugging in your electric barbecue starter and other appliances?

Are there outdoor faucets for washing the car and watering the lawn? If there is an underground sprinkling system for the lawn, turn it on (unless the ground is frozen). Does it function? Is the water flow strong at farthest extreme of the system, or is the stream too weak to reach all the areas it is supposed to cover?

If a member of your family or any of your friends have disabilities, is there access for them in their wheelchairs?

Is there a swimming pool or tennis court? Are they in good condition? In both cases, the visible surfaces should be smooth and unbroken. Most localities require fences around a pool—is there one? Does the liner show any signs of damage that might mean a leak? Bulging or uneven pool walls can indicate expensive trouble in the original preparation of a pool site. Check the filters and the general condition of the pumping area. It is a good sign if careful attention has been paid to keeping the pool clean.

In some communities, a pool or a tennis court can add significantly to the value of a home; however, make sure you are paying for something that won't cost you a good deal in maintenance or headaches after you have closed. If there is no pool or tennis court but you plan to have one installed, determine what the zoning requirements are in the municipality. There may be limitations as to location and specifications for construction that can make the process less appealing or more expensive.

THE NEIGHBORHOOD

While this book cannot pretend to be an all-inclusive primer on real estate investment, the inspection process must nevertheless include at least a moment's consideration of the neighborhood and its relationship to your safety and comfort, as well as its impact upon the value of your home.

First of all, is it a safe neighborhood? Are the streets neat and well maintained, or does the municipal government care a little less about this area than the one on the other side of the tracks with a higher tax base?

Does it appear that your neighbors-to-be take care of their yards and homes? One homeowner we know in New Jersey moved in before he ever glanced over into his next-door neighbor's yard. Then he found out that the guy next door moonlighted as an auto body repairman, and that the fellow always had cars in various states of disrepair and disassembly strewn across the yard, along with the paraphernalia of his trade, which involved spray painting and other noisy and messy tasks.

Are there streetlights? Is the house on a busy thoroughfare or a dead-end street? Not only is traffic dangerous to pets and children, but it can be loud and interfere with sleeping and other life patterns. Is there public transportation and how close is it to the home? If it is not within walking distance, is there adequate parking near the closest bus or train stop? What are the municipal services? Garbage pickup? Street cleaning?

If your children will or already do attend public schools, you should investigate the local system. The physical plant, the academic ratings, the ratio of collegebound to general students, and other issues are all important. Are there public playgrounds nearby? On the other hand, you may want to avoid a home too close to a school because of the congestion and noise that is inevitable with the coming and going of the students.

Look at the other houses in the vicinity. Are they much like the one you are considering, or significantly less desirable? Bigger or smaller, newer or older? Have they been maintained as well or better than the one you are looking at? Remember, it is rare for a house to be a great deal more valuable than the neighborhood average. Particularly if you plan to make major improvements in the house with the hope of making a handsome profit upon resale, you should make it your business to know the recent selling prices of a handful of nearby houses.

If you see any neighbors on your inspection tour or on any other visit, engage them in conversation. Ask them if they like the neighborhood, what their biggest gripe is, if there are any proposed power lines, generating plants, or major developments, commercial or residential, expected in the area.

POLLUTION CONCERNS

If you already live in the vicinity, you probably know about the condition of the air, but if not, check it out. The local government probably has an agency in charge of environmental protection, and it will answer your questions.

One question it probably can't answer, however, is about noise pollution in your particular location. Unless you plan to be housebound with the windows closed and the air conditioner running full-time, you will be subject to the noises of your neighbors. Are there dogs? Is there any commercial real estate nearby that will make noise anytime, but particularly in the evening, nights, or early mornings? Odors, too, should be a concern: manufacturing or agricultural activity, whether right next door or within the range of a light breeze, can make life unpleasant indeed.

ASSESSMENT OF CHECKPOINT NO. 1

MISCELLANEOUS CONCERNS: Aside from issues of safety, this is perhaps the most subjective checkpoint on the inspection tour. Do you like what you found? It seems to be a rule of human nature that it is a great deal easier to live with the bad news about your new home when you know about it up front and decide to accept it than when you move in, discover it, and have no choice—so acknowledge the bad news, absorb it, and then make your decision.

IMMEDIATE IMPROVEMENT INDEX: Matters of safety dominate the index in the yard. The following problems require your immediate attention:

I — Fences that are so rotted they are dangerous to anyone who leans on them;

— Hazardously protruding hanging branches (especially dead ones);

— An absence of nighttime light on the front walk;

— Any other small hazards to you or your guests that can be repaired with a minimum of materials and effort.

II — A craggy old tree that is unsound and endangers the house (its nearness to the house implies the expert services of a tree surgeon are required);

— The need for the installation of a substantial retaining wall (one twenty-five feet or more in length) because of significant erosion on a steep slope would most likely also cost in excess of two hundred dollars.

III — Short of a major landscaping job occasioned by a flood eroding a great crevice in the front lawn, there are no very expensive improvements that are likely to demand immediate attention at this checkpoint, although there are many, very expensive landscaping or other improvements that you might make by choice, including the installation of a pool or tennis court, both of which would probably cost in excess of ten thousand dollars.

WALK-AWAY FACTORS: A major polluter in the neighborhood is an important Walk-Away Factor. If the location of your house is in a low-lying area in a damp climate, standing water is evident on the property, and no additional drainage is available, that, too, is a Walk-Away Factor.

Checkpoint No. 2

EXTERNAL
WALL COVERINGS

Having looked at the surroundings of the house, turn your attention to the "skin" of the building itself, the external wall coverings.

It is at this checkpoint that you will begin to understand more clearly the discipline of inspecting the house itself. You must erase from your mind whatever your first generalized impressions of the walls were ("They seemed fine" or "I like the color"). Such impressions are important to instinctive distinctions ("Yes, I could live here" or "Oh, I'll have to repaint first thing") but they are not helpful in the assessment task. Your goal at this checkpoint, as elsewhere, is to identify the materials used, and to evaluate their quality and condition.

Is the surface of the house, or "siding," as it is known in the building trades, made of wood, brick, stone, aluminum, asphalt shingles, or some other material? Tap it with your finger to confirm your visual impression. If the siding is wood, is it shingles (thin strips of wood whose textured, visible surface is usually less than a half inch thick and of various widths, from a few inches to as much as a foot), horizontal clapboards (thicker, smoother lumber usually of ten or more feet in length), large panels (generally four- by eight-foot sheets), or vertical boards, often with narrower boards covering the cracks between the wider ones, a style called board-and-batten?

Just as no house is perfect, no building material lasts forever, but generally the longevity of these materials, longest to shortest, is likely to be brick and stone; cedar clapboard; cedar shingles; board finishes. Sellers of aluminum siding claim it lasts virtually forever, but that depends upon how well you can tolerate its tendency to fade towards colorlessness. Let's take each of the surfaces independently.

MASONRY

A mason's basic materials are stone or brick or similar blocks, with a binding material of mortar. The mortar is usually made of sand, water, cement, and lime.

Look closely at the surface of the masonry. Is its surface uniform? Are there signs of wear and tear, like chinks of missing mortar? Pay special attention to the side most exposed to the weather as this is where the damage is most likely to be found.

Look for loose and crumbling mortar down low and up high, and especially behind any vines that may be growing up the side of the house. Beautiful as the ivy covering may be, the vines have little tentacles that reach into tiny cracks, holding on for dear life as they make for the sky. In the process, those little cracks get bigger, and water gets in, freezes in the winter, and the cracks grow bigger still.

Numerous cracks and gaps in the lines of mortar mean that the walls will have to be repointed. Repointing simply means that the mortar has to be replaced. Doing so involves scraping out some of the remaining mortar so that the new mortar will have enough surface (roughly a half-inch depth) to hold to. The process is time-consuming and, therefore, expensive when performed by a professional. (The Rookie or Apprentice would be wise to leave this work to the experienced Handyman and the professionals.) Even if there are no evident gaps, test the mortar with your fingernail; if it is the consistency of dirt, it will also need repointing.

Is there a pattern of cracks, not just miscellaneous bits of missing mortar, but fissures that suggest a parting of one portion of the wall from another? Usually such cracks will zigzag like a staircase from one course (horizontal row) of bricks to the next. Serious cracking generally means a shifting of the foundation beneath, so make a note on your Checksheet to follow up on Checkpoint 6 if you find such a patterned crack. This generally means serious trouble—it's a Walk-Away Factor, especially in a house that is less than ten years old.

Often when the wall of a house is a combination of masonry and wood, the bricks form a "veneer wall." In that case, the bricks or stones are not load-bearing, but rather the wood frame wall within carries the weight of the house, and the bricks assume only their own. "Weep holes" should be left in the wall to allow water that might accumulate to drain. Weep holes are simply gaps between the bricks. If there are none, look again for cracks and bulges. If they, too, are absent and the house is more than five years old, you should have nothing to worry about.

Masonry is commonly plagued by efflorescence. The result of soluble salts in the bricks migrating to the surface of a wall along with water that has seeped in, efflorescence appears as a whitish powder. It does not indicate structural problems within the wall and can usually be eliminated with the application of a dilute solution of muriatic acid with a wire brush.

CLAPBOARDS, SHINGLES, BOARD-AND-BATTEN

If the siding is wood, look closely for peeling and flaking paint. Except for cedar or redwood boards, paint is essential to protect the wood against the prolonged exposure to the elements and to prevent decay.

Check for blistering and cracking on the surface, too. In itself, painting can be an expensive and time-consuming process, but if the wood beneath the present coat of paint seems to have deteriorated to the degree that it will require surface preparation or, worse yet, replacement, the time and costs increase precipitously.

It is rot that most often leads to the need for clapboards to be replaced. Can you see any signs of dampness? Look closely at the first piece of wood up from the ground. It should be a minimum of six to eight inches from the soil, with the foundation material (cement or stone or brick) separating it from the earth. (If the wood is flush to the ground or some portions of it are buried, go to Checkpoints 6 and 7 immediately. Serious rot and termite problems can be the direct result of such construction and will require that you make immediate repairs.)

If you suspect rot trouble wield your screwdriver like a knife and jab it into the wood closest to the ground. Try not to gouge great, unsightly holes, and don't mar perfectly healthy clapboards. Probe the wood all around the house this way. If the screwdriver penetrates easily in a number of places, you have come across a Walk-Away Factor. More likely, there will be no more than one or two areas that have decayed over time. They must be dealt with in short order but, if confined to a small area, will not require a major investment.

If you see signs of mold on the siding, that suggests a mildew that results from too little sunlight rather than rot. Usually, the siding will not decay, and the mold can be removed from a painted surface with bleach and water.

If your house has wooden shingles on the outside, you should check for cracked, broken, or missing shingles. (The words "shingle" and "shake" are often used interchangeably, but, in fact, shakes are split from the tree while shingles are sawed; the shakes have a more textured appearance, tend to be thicker, and have a longer life expectancy.)

Look for "cupping" or warping of the shingles (and shakes) as another sign of their advancing age. Some cupping is to be expected in shingles that are twenty or more years old. But if a quarter or more of the shingles are evidently warping, if some are breaking down and ready to fall off, replacement may be necessary. This is labor for an advanced Handyman and rates a *III* on the Immediate Improvement Index.

If there are brown, vertical stains that seem to come from beneath each layer of siding, the cause is most likely rusting iron (rather than aluminum or galvanized) nails. There's not a great deal you can do without spending a great deal, so living with it is the usual solution. It may not be attractive, but it presents no danger to the safety or structural integrity of the house. But it does suggest that the builder saved a few dollars unwisely, so other shortcuts may also be found in the house's construction.

Cedar is decay resistant, so painting cedar shingles is not essential. However, cedar's life expectancy is increased, and the chances of cracking and sizing variations over time is substantially decreased, when it is sealed with paint or coated with a preservative. Most wooden shingles are of red cedar, though redwood and cypress are also used.

Other sorts of wooden finishes include hardboard siding (made of bonded wood fibers), plywood panels (exterior grade plywood, made of veneers bonded with a waterproof glue), and individual boards. These sidings are generally hung vertically to facilitate the flow of water down and away. They should be inspected for signs of water damage (peeling paint, discoloration) and at the joints between one section and another. You should be alert here, too, for rot and warping. As with shingles, replacement of badly deteriorated panels or boards is for the skilled Handyman.

Note that vines are potentially harmful to wood siding as well as brick, since they can cause the wood hidden by them to deteriorate and may also provide termites with a means of support for their tunnels. Inspect carefully behind and below the vines.

ALUMINUM AND OTHER SIDINGS

Aluminum siding requires less maintenance than some of the other wall coverings, as it does not require painting. It also does not rot or rust, even when its baked enamel surface is scratched. Consequently, the concern with aluminum siding in general is cosmetic. We've seen one house sided in aluminum where one entire wall was virtually covered with dents and pitting: there were three boys in the family, and they used the adjacent yard for playing all sorts of sports. As a result, the wall became a backstop for softballs, footballs, and golf balls.

When looking at aluminum or vinyl siding, look for missing or loose pieces, and dents and scratches. To the eye, vinyl siding is indistinguishable from aluminum. It does flex when touched, however. As with aluminum, check for cracks and missing or loose pieces. Also, press the siding in several places two feet or so above the ground. If you feel the material underneath (it is usually wood) to be weak or crumbling, it may be rotten.

In rare cases, the aluminum siding may not even cover the original siding. One couple we know in Concord, Massachusetts, was shocked to find that beneath the aluminum on their early eighteenth-century saltbox the clapboard siding had been removed, so restoring the house to its original appearance involved not only removing the aluminum but installing an entirely new surface of clapboards. Ordinarily, aluminum or vinyl siding that is retrofitted to an older home is applied over the extant siding, which adds strength and rigidity to the newer, more flexible siding.

Other sidings like asbestos cement shingles (brittle sheets of fiberglass or an organic felt material covered with granules) and stucco (which looks like textured plaster) resist the onslaught of Mother Nature extremely well; they are quite durable and are of no interest to termites. As a result, your concern should be for damaged or missing portions rather than for weathering or wear.

Asbestos cement shingles, like roofing shingles, can be replaced at reasonable cost, though matching the weathered color of the old shingles with new ones is difficult and the result can be an unsightly variation in the appearance of your home. Stucco is also extremely durable and relatively easy to repair. If it develops cracks, they must be sealed, but this can be done with a cement paint in the case of small cracks, or a mortar-base mixture when cracks larger than one sixteenth of an inch occur. Substantial sections or pieces that have or are about to come free from the side of the house suggest that all but the most energetic Handyman should walk away or commit to an expensive rehabilitation project.

OPENINGS AND CLOSINGS

Whatever material was used for siding on the house, look closely at the openings in the walls. Windows and doors require a transition from one material to another, and as we will see again and again trouble—especially leakage—is most often found at such transition points.

Look at the caulking in the joints. Caulk is a substance rather like chewing gum that, when moist, can be applied with a gunlike tool. It goes on in a bead (like toothpaste squeezed from a tube) and when it dries, it hardens into a watertight seal. There are several different kinds of caulk (including latex/acrylic-, oil-, and silicone-base varieties) that have differing price tags and advantages. Silicone base is the best but, given its cost, you will probably find the acrylic or latex most suitable for exterior applications. Recaulking is a job an Apprentice should find easy to learn; an energetic Rookie willing to screw up his courage could also master the technique. An inexpensive gun and a tube of caulk can be purchased for less than ten dollars.

Make sure the caulking is tight around the windows and doors and trim. Check the joints between the siding and the foundation, as well as at any other place dissimilar materials meet. The caulk should not be brittle or broken, nor should there be any gaps that would allow water to enter or to remain; remember, a primary purpose of the skin of the dwelling is to shed rain and other moisture.

Are there any signs of discoloration on the wood around the windows? If the window frames are metal, is there any rust? If so, note it on your Checksheet under Checkpoint 16, when we'll look at the problem from the inside.

Inspect all corners for rot and make sure they are caulked tightly closed. Corners are often less watertight than they should be. Inside corners as well as outside corners must be checked (if you were inside a cube, all the corners around you would be inside corners; outside the cube, only exterior corners would be visible).

LEVELS AND SQUARES

We'll look at the windows and doors closely from the inside, but for now step back from the house and look at the openings: Are they square, or do they look like they have shifted? In an eighteenth-century wood frame colonial, you should expect things to be a little off square. Many people, in fact, see this as part of the charm of an old house and testimony to its extreme age. But in newer construction, it is less quaint and more worrisome.

To a carpenter, a level and a square are essential tools. But for an inspection, you can usually trust your eye to be your guide. Go to a corner on one of the longer sides of the house and eye its length: Does the wall run straight to the next corner, or are there bulges? Do this from all sides.

Step back and look at the house ground-to-roofline: Again, do you see wavy lines, or are only straight lines apparent? If you do see undulating lines, make a note on your Checksheet and we'll follow up when we get to Checkpoint 6. Bulges can be signs of serious structural problems, and they are most often detected down under your house where Mother Earth offers her support (and sometimes withdraws her offer, too). If the house has a masonry veneer wall, look at it carefully from a sidelong vantage, as the veneer wall is most often constructed an inch or so away from the wood frame of the house and linked to it by metal ties. Sometimes over the passage of time the ties corrode, and the wall can bulge.

A likely problem area is the juncture of the walls and the roofline. Look for signs that water has been confined in the walls. This presents a serious problem for any siding, but in the case of stucco it can lead to serious cracking and fissures on the surface. Any painted surface will start cracking and blistering if water gets behind it, and wooden shingles and clapboards alike will cup; panels often will warp or even lose their first layer of laminate.

ASSESSMENT OF CHECKPOINT NO. 2

MISCELLANEOUS CONCERNS: The bottom-line determinations at this checkpoint are essentially two. First, is the siding material in good condition, or will you have to invest labor and dollars to make it weathertight? Second, do you note any problems with the windows or doors or any indication of uneven settlement? If you found any of these concerns, make sure you noted them for followup on your Checksheet.

IMMEDIATE IMPROVEMENT INDEX: The following problems merit mention on the Index:

I — Efflorescence on brick walls;
   — Broken-down caulking around a window or two or on the corners;
   — Peeling or blistering paint in a few small, confined areas.

II — Repointing a portion of one side of a brick house;

— Replacing a few siding boards or panels on one side of the house;

— Peeling or blistering paint in numerous substantial areas;

— The need to recaulk a great many windows and corners and the indication of some decay problems;

— Patching a few cracks in stucco.

III — Re-siding one or more sides of the house;

— Repointing the entire house;

— Restuccoing one whole side of the house;

— If the paint on the siding is peeling and blistering and the entire house needs painting;

— If there is evidence of some rot in more than one small, confined area of the wall.

WALK-AWAY FACTORS: Chronic cracking in a zigzag staircase pattern in masonry walls is a definite Walk-Away Factor, especially if it is not confined to a small area in one wall. The origin of the problem is most likely in the foundation but will require both structural work downstairs and extensive corrective masonry work aboveground.

Another Walk-Away Factor is uneven settling, most clearly evidenced by serious bulges in a brick veneer wall, deep sags in the roofline, out-of-plumb walls, or evident shifting of walls or sections of the house with respect to others indicated by gaps at joints or corners or a visible misalignment of the pieces. If you find these signs or if the house is of recent construction and many elements seem off-square, walk away.

If the wood siding begins at ground level (or below), rather than being at least six inches above the soil, this virtually guarantees trouble, either at the present time or in the near future. Follow up this observation at Checkpoints 6 and 7 before making your determination, but chances are this, too, is a Walk-Away Factor.

Chronic cracking on all sides of a stucco house (a number of cracks greater than one sixteenth of an inch wide) means serious trouble, too, perhaps in more than just the surface of the stucco, as water has probably entered the walls and damaged not only the stucco but the structure within as well. Extensive indications of this kind also constitute a Walk-Away Factor.

Checkpoint No. 3

INDOOR/OUTDOOR SPACES

Porches first became commonplace in the Victorian Age; elevated off the damp ground, the porch was an exterior social space that could take good advantage of cooling breezes yet offer some of the comforts of a living room. In our time the same instinct for indoor/outdoor spaces has led to the construction of decks that are immediately accessible from the kitchen or other interior living spaces.

Whatever the age of the house, a deck or a porch is probably a selling point. An indoor/outdoor space is not strictly necessary in most climates but can be a big plus for hot summer evenings or entertaining on Saturday afternoons. But by their very nature, decks and porches are exposed to the elements and are more likely to have decay and other problems than other living areas.

In the case of one New York City couple, the house's problem was with its deck. Anne and Bill Johnson's house was a rustic weekend cottage, a perfect escape from their hectic business lives in the city. It was perched high on a cliff, and the attached deck looked into the tops of the trees, giving them the illusion of being in a bird's nest, looking down at the forest floor below.

The problem was that when it rained, the water poured off the roof onto the deck. Unfortunately, that also meant that water flowed into the wooden structure of the walls, too, because the deck was attached directly to the house. But Bill and Anne were lucky to catch it early; the damage was minimal, and the cure very simple: they installed a gutter and a downspout to direct the water elsewhere.

As you can see from the Johnsons' experience, water is, as usual, the chief troublemaker, whether it's on the ground or falling from the sky. Remember that so-called dry rot will occur wherever water does not naturally run off. On the walls and roof of a house, gravity's pull usually is sufficient to draw away the moisture, but in the case of decks and porches, with their horizontal designs, water can accumulate at low points. This is why porches are usually built with a slope that encourages gravity to do its work and draw the rain off to the ground nearby. Only rarely are decks designed with such slopes.

Water isn't the only potential villain at this checkpoint. Termites and carpenter ants and large pests like various members of the rodent family also find comfortable nesting places in these outdoor spaces, in particular, underneath them. To complicate matters still further, water and insect and animal problems under the deck or porch frequently are not confined to their starting places; the termite that finds congenial hunting grounds in the deck beams may well move into the attached house.

This checkpoint is one at which problems are frequently found, but the hours of labor involved in rebuilding these areas are usually fewer and the materials less varied and less expensive than in interior spaces. A Handyman will probably feel comfortable taking on most any task relating to this checkpoint, while an Apprentice should be able to make minor repairs when necessary.

It is important that close attention be paid to the problems at this checkpoint, as they can signal trouble to come within the house. If you find indications that porch or deck deterioration has led to problems within adjacent portions of the house, you may not be so lucky as Anne and Bill, and you may have met up with this checkpoint's lone Walk-Away Factor. Serious trouble in both the outdoor space and in the structure of attached portions of the house suggest walking away may be your wisest choice. But we will talk more of the signs of these problems as we discuss decks and porches individually.

DECKS

Unless the deck is clearly unsteady, you should begin your inspection topside. Walk around the perimeter of the deck (or decks). Listen for creaks and groans. Do any portions of the decking spring as you walk on them? Is there any cracking or evident rot? Are there any loose or missing boards?

Make sure you crisscross the deck as well. If you find any symptoms of softness, note where they are. Count the number of boards from the edge or by some other means establish the location of the weakness so that when you go beneath the deck you can find the same spots and look at them from there.

Is there a gap between each of the floorboards? There should be approximately a quarter inch, so rainwater can run off. If there is none, check even more carefully for rot problems; there may be none, but the odds are higher that there will be some signs of softness or decay.

If the deck is painted, remember it will have to be

repainted every few years. If the paint is very recent, make sure it isn't obscuring some rot that will soon show itself again. The best method of checking this is to stab the wood with your screwdriver as you did at Checkpoint 2. If the blade penetrates more than a quarter of an inch, there is probably some softness present. Note this on your Checksheet for follow up when inspecting the deck from below.

Check the guardrails around the edge. Is there any give? There shouldn't be. Are they strong enough for 250-pound Uncle Harry to lean on after he's had a couple of strong ones some Saturday afternoon in August? If the deck is more than a foot or two off the ground, is there a sufficient amount of protection between the posts in the guardrails to prevent small children—yours or your guests' —from tumbling through? Simple guardrail construction and repairs are within the reach of a willing Apprentice, though if the finish carpentry of the deck is very decorative, with elaborate moldings or shapes used, it may be better left to the Handyman.

Now, go underneath. If you can't actually walk beneath, either crawl under or reach in as best you can from the outside. A general perception comes first: Does everything seem to be as straight as it should be? It's important that the support be even and constant, so if one leg or another looks out of kilter, pay special attention to it as you continue your inspection. Lean on each side of the deck, and push on it with the weight of your body. If there is any give, think twice about heading under it. It should be solid.

At the base of each leg should be a footing. What is it made of? If the leg itself is made of wood and is submerged in the ground, that could mean trouble: wooden porch and deck legs can provide a virtual freeway for termites and other insects. The legs should be on concrete footings that extend below the frost line; installing concrete footings requires jacking of the deck and is probably best left to the well-equipped Handyman with experience dealing with jacks and building concrete forms. If there are footings there already, check them for signs of cracking or shifting.

What is the deck made of? The most often used material these days is pressure-treated lumber, as we saw in inspecting patios in Checkpoint 1. Pressure-treated lumber is impregnated with a strong preservative to provide long-lasting protection against decay and insect infestation; it has a much greater life expectancy than wood that is untreated or merely dipped or coated with a preservative. Redwood and cedar decks are a good deal more expensive, but they have nature's equivalent of pressure treating and are also resistant to decay.

Check the posts that support the deck. In addition to being vertical, are they sound? Hit them firmly with the heel of your hand or a hammer. Are they bearing weight from above or do they swing free? If they swing free, that suggests bad design or construction. Make a note on your Checksheet.

Check the beams and floor joists that support the planks on the deck above. The beams are the large, often square supports that extend horizontally, linking the posts; the floor joists are smaller, often $2'' \times 6''$ or $2'' \times 8''$ dimension lumber, set on top of the beams and the floorboards are nailed to them.

Be sure the deck has maintained its square shape: Do the joists dip between the legs that support them? Look down the length of the joists to check this. Are you looking at straight lines, or is there sagging? If there is a noticeable sag, it would be wise to add another vertical post at the low point(s). Again, this will require jackings and mixing concrete and is probably for the Handyman.

Look for rot in all the wooden members. Use your screwdriver to stab at the joists and beams and legs. If the tool penetrates more than a small fraction of an inch, this indicates dry rot. Decayed wood is the single most common reason for rebuilding a deck: signs of decay in more than two or three isolated areas of the deck indicate that the time has come for an investment in materials and labor to replace at least the badly decayed wood or, more likely, to rebuild the bulk of the deck.

If the deck is attached to the house—especially if there are no legs on the house side of the deck and the house bears the weight of the deck—check to see how the deck is attached. The fasteners should be lag bolts, which are, essentially, large screws. Lag bolts can usually be identified by their heads: rather than being rounded like nail heads, they are square or hexagonal so they can be tooled into the wood with a wrench.

If lag bolts were not used, is the deck separating from the house? If not, estimate the age of the deck from the condition of the wood and paint: if it has been there several years and hasn't separated, it probably won't, even without the lag bolts. But lag bolts should be installed in a new deck. An Apprentice with an electric drill (to predrill the holes to prevent splitting) and a heavy-duty adjustable wrench can take on this task.

Examine the nails, too; a good builder will have used coated nails that will not rust. Untreated nails will reveal themselves by streaks of rust. While this will not significantly weaken the deck, the presence of numerous cracks or splits in the wood around nails or bolts can weaken both the lumber and the bond between it and the member to which it is attached. A pattern of many cracks and splits means some reconstruction is in order.

PORCHES

Inspecting a porch involves much the same concerns as does a deck inspection, only the underside is often less accessible. Begin your porch inspection by walking a few dozen feet away from the house. Turn to face the house and eye the porch with respect to the rooflines. Do you see parallel lines? If there is an evident sag, you should begin your inspection of the porch at the lowest point of the sag.

As with the deck, you must look at the floor from above and below and walk it thoroughly. The supporting legs, beams, and joists as well as floorboards must be probed and pushed and examined. The balustrade, as well, is crucial. Remember, too, if the house is a handsome old home with numerous decorative elements like turned supports for the railing or fancy, band-sawed gingerbread around the borders of the porch, replacement of these elements can be very expensive, requiring hand remaking of the individual parts and tools that even a well-equipped Handyman is unlikely to have.

If the construction of your porch incorporates a solid, waist-high wall around the outside, inspect carefully at its base. If it is flush to the floor, it is a perfect location for water to amass and to cause the wood to decay. Even if there is no sign of dry rot, the boards may have been replaced recently. If the wall is flush to the floor, are there weep holes (small gaps at floor level) to allow the water to run off?

Look at the point of intersection between the porch and the walls of the home. Sometimes water, and eventually dry rot, will work their way from the porch to the frame or foundation of the house. If you see any signs of this (check with your probe for softness, above and below), make careful note and follow up when we get to Checkpoint 6.

As most porches also have roofs, check the roof and its supports from the inside of the porch. Are they solid? Use the heel of your hand to hammer the post (gently at first, harder if it seems sound) to test their soundness. Is there any apparent sign of deterioration? Wood that has lost its paint and taken on a grayish, soft appearance no doubt is decayed. Be sure to look at the roof of the porch at Checkpoint 4.

ASSESSMENT OF CHECKPOINT NO. 3

MISCELLANEOUS CONCERNS: Your final determination regarding the indoor/outdoor space (if any) in the house concerns three basic issues: its solidity, safety, and its appropriateness to your needs. You should therefore determine whether or not the porches and/or decks are structurally sound; whether the design is safe, complete with guardrails for large and small guests alike; and whether the deck or porch is a practical and attractive extra, or whether it is inconveniently located, too small, or simply unappealing.

IMMEDIATE IMPROVEMENT INDEX: The following deck or porch problems demand your immediate attention:

   I — A small deck more than a foot off the ground that has no guardrail around it;

      — A painted deck that shows signs of needing to be repainted (peeling or blistered paint, areas where the paint has simply been worn through). This is a task a Rookie can reasonably take on.

II — A large deck more than a foot off the ground
with no guardrail;

— Signs of some deterioration in the floorboards in
a confined portion of the deck;

— The deck is apparently sound but the wooden
posts that support it are in contact with the
ground. The deck should be jacked up temporar-
ily and concrete footing poured beneath the
posts to prevent decay and insect damage;

— Evidence of some sagging of the floor joists mean
that additional support posts should be added.

III — Signs of structural weakness in the deck indicate
it must be rebuilt. Cracked or broken supporting
posts are one sign of this; another is if the whole
deck sways when you lean your shoulder into
one side of it;

— Extensive indications of deterioration or decay
in the deck or porch's supporting structure, especially the posts or beams that carry its weight.

WALK-AWAY FACTORS: A deck or porch that is a di-
saster area and that will require complete reconstruction
certainly rates a III on the Index. If, however, that badly
deteriorated porch is attached to the house; if portions of
the adjacent house nearby also show signs of serious deterioration, it is important that you follow up carefully when
inspecting the foundation of the house and checking for
termites. Virtually every deck or porch will require serious
rebuilding periodically but when significant portions of the
house do as well, it may be time to walk away.

THE ROOF

The single most important line of defense between you and the elements is the roof. Its broad expanse is exposed to precipitation and the sun's rays; it can protect you, or not, depending on how well it was constructed and whether or not it has been properly maintained.

Ideally, you should be blissfully unaware of your roof once you move in. It is unlikely that your guests will offer admiring remarks like "Oh, what a handsome roof!" In short, if you find yourself conscious of it, that generally means trouble.

Any assessment of the roof largely concerns materials; how good are they and how old? In the case of a roof, the qualitative differences between materials is more evident than any other place. Exposed to the elements as the roof is, its wear and tear is greater than any other portion of the house.

Before we look at the roof, be warned: although the best place to inspect the roof is on top of it, the roof is the most dangerous place to be in the average house. This is particularly true with pitched roofs, but flat roofs are dangerous too, especially those with little or no parapet wall that extends above the edge of the roof. It is safest for you to stay on the ground, and step back from the house far enough to see the surface of the roof. Look up from below while walking around the house and checking each side. A pair of binoculars may allow you to make nearly as detailed an inspection as you would on the roof itself.

If you are of a mind to wander up onto the roof, talk yourself out of it if you are not confident of your balance. If you are not experienced at climbing ladders, don't, especially if the ladder at hand is rickety or weak. If the roof is wet from a recent rain, get the best vantage you can from the ground and inspect from there; the only thing more dangerous than a pitched roof is a wet one. And if you decide to go up anyway, watch your step, don't swing your ladder into the electric or telephone wires, and don't be ashamed to get down on all fours to assure your balance.

When it comes to repairs, given the height (and therefore danger) involved, in general the roof is better left to professional ministrations if you are at all squeamish about heights or inexperienced with ladders and tricky footing. It is not that the skills required are difficult, however; in fact shingling is relatively easy to learn and a number of useful publications are available to show you how. Handymen and even a few Apprentices may well be up to taking on some of the roofing repairs.

LOOKING UP

In any case, your first concern is best studied from below. Begin with the south and southwestern exposures of the house, as they are subject to more weathering. We've seen houses where the north face looked virtually new while on the south side of the same gable the roof leaked badly. The sun, the wind, and precipitation exact a considerable toll over time.

As you look at the roof from a groundbound vantage some distance away, do you see any sagging? Is the roofline straight? If there is a sag, it could indicate a number of different structural problems. Note on your Checksheet under Checkpoint 11 to follow up on the variations in the roofline when you are inspecting the attic. Serious structural problems within a roof can be a Walk-Away Factor, so check out any such indications very carefully.

Does the chimney, if there is one, aim straight for the sky, or is there an apparent tilt? If so, there could be problems with its foundation, and we'll follow this up in Checkpoint 6 and Checkpoint 13.

Look for signs of shingles added since the construction of the house. If there is a clear difference between the shingles in adjacent areas, it may suggest some patching has been done to repair some problem or other, like a large tree limb falling, or a chimney fire. Make a note to check the interior if you find any such signs. It is also possible that the patch was applied because the roof had begun to leak at that point; this suggests, unfortunately, that the entire roof is probably going to require resurfacing in the near future. We will talk more about that later when we discuss the various roofing surfaces.

If you do walk on the roof, you should also note any areas that are soft or flex underfoot as you walk around, and follow this up at Checkpoint 11.

In areas of the country where the thermometer falls below freezing for any length of time in the winter, you should look carefully for signs of water damage where the roof overhangs. The downhill edges of the shingles may appear to be separating from the shingles beneath. This, along with grayish brown water stains or peeling paint in the fascia board (the board facing out immediately beneath the first course of shingles) or the soffit (the downward-facing portion of the eave up underneath the overhang of the cornice), suggests that ice dams may occur.

Ice dams result from snow and ice that melts farther up the roof; the water drips down and refreezes on the eave where the temperature is cooler (it's farther from the heated interior). Ice dams may cause melting water to back up beneath the shingles and leak into the house, running down walls or ruining ceilings. They can be prevented by running specially designed electrical cables, or installing flashing on the eaves. These are tasks for the Handyman who is equipped with ladders and scaffolding for proper access to the roof.

FLASHING

Other than the surface of the roof itself, the most important single ingredient of any roof structure is the flashing. Flashing consists of thin sheets of metal—copper is best, aluminum more common—that are applied to angles and curves and variations in a roof surface where the principal roofing material, which is generally less flexible, cannot provide a weathertight fit. In the case of most shingles, they will bend but would tear or break if they were to be, say, bent to fit a ninety-degree joint. Flashing is used in such circumstances.

Inspect the flashing carefully. It is also found at the edges of the roof, and around chimneys, vent pipes, dormers, and other projections that break the planes of the roof. Look for signs of wear and tear: when flashing ceases to do its job, particularly if it is in a strategic position, like the valley between the two roof surfaces linking an ell to the main house, the holes in it can act much like a drain, delivering rainwater in a torrent to the roof members and attic. Look for holes, cracks, and sloppy installation. If you spy flashing that appears to be leaking (the connection of the chimney to the house is one common trouble spot), be sure to follow up inside the house and look for signs of leakage there.

Remember, it is at the transition points where trouble is likely to be found, so pay as close attention as your vantage will allow to the peak of the roof, to the valleys, to any other intersection points where different planes meet.

The most common repair made to leaking flashing is the application of tarlike substances. This is inexpensive and can be applied by even a cautious Rookie who is willing to climb onto the roof and wield a brush to apply it. The material may have a petroleum, asphalt, or other base. (Note that the presence of large quantities of the black, clotted stuff already on the flashing suggests previous repairs.) Be forewarned that it doesn't last forever and, in fact, may cause the flashing to erode more quickly, so you should expect that further repairs will be necessary later on. It is satisfactory only as a short-term solution.

The replacement of whole sections of flashing usually involves replacing nearby shingles as well; a complete reroofing will involve replacing all the flashing. Both of these are at least into Handyman territory and, given the need for ladders and specialized equipment, may best be left to roofing contractors.

SLATE ROOFS

Slate doesn't last forever, but it can last for a century or more, even in challenging climates like New England's. Today, slate roofs are too expensive for most of us to install, but many older homes we can afford still feature the carefully quarried, stratified stone on their roofs.

Even if you have the balance and confidence of a steeplejack do not—repeat, *do not*—try to walk on a slate roof. You'll almost certainly do it damage, as the stones are thin and brittle, even if they were installed yesterday.

Look for cracked or chipped or broken shingles. Look for places where pieces have broken away. Repairs on slate roofs are best left to the expert; be forewarned that experts in slate roofing are not easy to come by, however, and their time may be expensive.

A slate roof on an old house that is still square indicates a very strong house frame beneath. However, a sagging slate roof may suggest expensive problems, since some slate roofs were applied to structures not designed to support their weight. If you find indications of this, follow it up in Checkpoint 11.

Tiled roofs look utterly different from slate roofs, but the problems and the concerns are essentially the same. Make sure the tiles are all there and intact.

CEDAR SHINGLES

Next to slate, cedar shingles or shakes are the longest-lasting roofing surface commonly found on residential buildings. As pointed out earlier, shingles are sawed, while shakes are split; the surface of shingles is smoother, shakes have a more textured look and feel.

Cedar shingles or shakes on a roof are the same as those on the walls of the building, save that usually they are applied in three rather than two layers. They are subject to the same kinds of problems as cedar siding, only more so: water runs off their flatter surface more slowly, the sun rests on the surface longer and more directly each day, and snow sometimes remains on the roof for months on end.

Cedar shingles can be expected to last roughly twenty-five years and shakes nearly twice that, depending in each case upon the rain and snowfall, the humidity, and the pitch of the roof. Red cedar is most commonly used, but white cedar, redwood, cypress, and other woods are occasionally used as shingling materials as well. Since wood is an organic material, wood shingles will rot if damp for prolonged periods, so look for fungus and mold, particularly on shaded or north-facing portions.

The older a shingled roof, the drier the shingles get. As the natural moisture dries out, the shingle will begin to cup, or curl. If a quarter or more of any section of the roof has begun to show these symptoms, you should anticipate having to reroof those portions shortly.

Reroofing any surface is expensive, even if you take on the task yourself. It is the province of the experienced and well-equipped Handyman. The job is also time-consuming so if you try and do it alone, you may find portions of your house without cover for some time, which is one of the advantages of using an experienced crew of roofers: they can do it quickly, and don't have to wait for the weekend to pick up where they left off.

If you decide to take on the reroofing yourself, do your homework first. Then begin with a small section to be sure you have made the right decision; don't get the whole old roof stripped first and then decide you want to hire an expert, as it may be some time before he is available.

ASPHALT SHINGLES

Asphalt shingles are the most common roofing surface in this country. Made by impregnating fiberglass or another medium with asphalt, the asphalt shingles are then given a surface of sandlike grains.

When inspecting asphalt shingles, look first for missing or damaged shingles. A strong wind may have blown some off, but the odds are that missing or damaged shingles indicate an older roof in need of replacement. One sign of aged shingles is the absence of the granules: they protect the fiberglass padding from the sun, while the medium beneath resists moisture. When the protective grains erode, the lower layer is more likely to curl.

Asphalt shingles have roughly a twenty-year life expectancy, depending upon the wear and tear of the climate. If the granules are gone and some curling is evident, replacement of the shingles is imminent. If replacement is or soon will be necessary, try to find an angle from which you can count the number of layers of shingles. There must be considerable overlap, so don't be deceived into thinking that there already are two layers of shingles on the house. But remember that standard practice allows only one reshingling of a roof before all the old shingles—both layers, that is—must be removed and new ones added.

The age of the house may also help you in making this determination. A ten-year-old house is unlikely to have been reshingled; one that is more than twenty-five years old almost certainly has been.

Asbestos cement shingles are quite different from asphalt shingles—instead of fiberglass or other base, they use asbestos fibers and portland cement as a base. Even so, their problems are similar. One added concern, however, is that asbestos cement shingles are more brittle than the others, and therefore are more likely to crack and break. Make an extra sweep of the roof with your binoculars to check for cracks. Numerous broken asbestos cement shingles indicate that reroofing time has come. Because of the cancer-causing nature of asbestos, only trained roofers should try and deal with the asbestos cement shingles.

FLAT ROOFS

Flat roofs are, in most parts of this country, more often characteristic of commercial than of residential buildings. But if the house you are thinking about buying has a flat roof, it, too, deserves close attention.

A flat roof on a building taller than a single story should be accessible from the interior; if it is not, that is a definite design lapse that suggests you should be extra vigilant in looking for other corners cut in the design and construction of the building.

Once you are on the roof, begin your inspection by looking for roof vents. We will discuss ventilation in detail when we come to the attic portion of the inspection, but in the case of flat roofs, ventilation is all important. The very nature of a flat roof encourages water to pool on its surface, and you should be alert for areas that have clearly had stagnant water sitting on them for extended periods. Puddles that remain for prolonged periods can encourage the breeding of insects, as well as cause the roofing material itself to deteriorate.

Next, look for runoffs. The design should allow for routes the water will follow to escape the roof. They can be as simple as the edge of the roof itself, or as complicated as drains in the middle of the roof that feed into an elaborate, interior downspout system. If either ventilation ports for the ceiling/roof area or runoff arrangements are missing, water or moisture problems are more likely, and you should follow up in the attic and upstairs area later in the inspection and be on the look out for signs of water damage. Be sure to mark this for follow-up on your Check-sheet.

Look at the surface carefully. Some flat roofs are made of sheet metal; more common is some combination of a rolled roofing material called "felt" (usually, it is an asphalt-saturated material) and a coal tar or asphalt pitch called bitumen that is applied as a liquid. Look for obvious tears and breaks in the surface, for sections where the surface layer is peeling away, and follow up inside to see if such imperfections have already led to water damage within. Also look for vapor pockets, irregular bubbles that indicate that water has gotten underneath the roof surface and vaporized. It means you have a leak.

CHIMNEYS

While you are inspecting the roof, take a careful look at the chimney(s). At Checkpoint 13 we will look in detail at the fireplaces, but clues gathered topside may guide you then.

Begin with the exterior of the chimney: Is the masonry sound? The same concerns discussed in Checkpoint 1 of brick and mortar condition are crucial here as well. Are any of the bricks or stones broken or loose? Is the mortar that binds them together deteriorating? Will it have to be repointed?

Look for efflorescence, the powdery presence of white, soluble salts that have been leached from the bricks by water. It can be cleaned relatively easily with a brush and muriatic acid (a task even a Rookie may want to take on), but the work will have to be done on the roof, dangerous for you or a professional.

Check the height of the chimney. The top should stand two or more feet above the peak of a pitched and three over a flat roof. If, however, the chimney is more than ten feet away from a higher roofline it is acceptable that it not be taller, although downdrafts are more likely under such circumstances.

If you are inspecting on the roof, look down the chimney. It should have a flue lining, one made of a fireproof substance. If you can clearly see the outlines of individual bricks rather than pipelike sections, the chimney is not lined. If that is the case, or there are apparent breaks or any signs of deterioration inside the flue, you would be well advised to consult a chimney expert, as these are fire hazards. In a chimney fire in an unlined flue, flames lick through any gaps and will ignite any combustibles within their reach in the attic or other adjacent interior areas. An unlined chimney, however, can be relined in place with a stainless steel flexible flue. An adventurous Handyman may be able to do the job, but in many communities the fire code requires either an inspection of the work or that it be done by an authorized professional. Check with the local fire department.

Often there are two or more flues in a chimney, as no single flue should vent more than one fireplace or furnace or boiler. Be sure to inspect each of them.

Is there a buildup of soot or other material in the flue? Note if one of the flues has a considerable accumulation of fine soot, since that can be a sign in houses heated with oil of an inefficient furnace. If you find this symptom, note it on your Checksheet and follow it up at Checkpoint 9. If the accumulation is coarser, and smells like a campfire after dousing, the accumulation is most likely a substance called creosote, the residue of a wood fire in a stove or fireplace. A common cause of chimney fires, creosote must be regularly removed from chimneys to prevent a dangerous buildup of the flammable material. A thick layer of creosote means the chimney should be thoroughly cleaned before it is used.

Is there a rain or drip cap on the chimney? The cap is most often made of mortar; whatever material it is made of, it is a pitched top to the chimney, designed to direct rainwater off the chimney and onto the roof around it. Without a drip cap or some other means of directing rain away from the chimney, the water will eventually enter the mortar between the bricks, freeze in cold weather, and cause the mortar to crack and deteriorate, requiring that the chimney be repointed.

SKYLIGHTS

As with the chimney, we'll have a follow-up look at the skylights when we go inside, but important observations are to be made from without. Look at the flashing in particular: Do there appear to be any gaps between the roof surface and the flashing around the skylight?

Skylights offer a remarkable volume of light, often to rooms where the walls are low and the windows scant. The same availability to sunlight suggests access for water and dampness as well. If there are any wood surfaces on the outside, look carefully for staining or deterioration. Look at the window and its flashing—and the roof immediately above it—and determine the "drip line," that is, the line water would follow, beckoned by gravity, off and away from the window. If there appear to be any low points on the skylight where water might pool, look there with extra care. Note any indications of leakage or decay on your Checksheet for follow-up at Checkpoint 16.

GUTTERS AND DOWNSPOUTS

In the Snowbelt gutters and downspouts can be a liability because of the maintenance required, but they will protect the ground below from eroding, can cut down on water in the basement, and can save soffit and facing trim from decay.

A variety of materials are used in making gutters and downspouts. Copper is the most expensive and will last the longest; aluminum is probably the most common, followed by galvanized and plastic materials.

The problems with each kind are much the same: over time Mother Nature wears away at the material and they all begin to leak. Look for missing pieces; check for rust in galvanized gutters. Copper, unlike other materials, is soldered at the joists and probably will not leak at those junctures. However, you should look up from below at the copper gutter to check for the tiny holes that will develop in its length over time.

Check for downspouts: you may not notice their absence, but if they are missing, the concentrated flow of water from an entire surface of the roof may accumulate on the ground immediately below, leading to the erosion of soil around the foundation and even decay if the rainwater enters the basement and comes into contact with the wood frame of the house.

Some older homes have box gutters, which are gutters built into the eaves. They must be inspected from the roof. Their interior waterways are usually lined with a waterproof material like copper or asphalt roll roofing. Maintenance is required of the latter lining, typically an application of asphalt cement every few years. Box gutters usually cannot be seen from the ground, but their design also means that when they fail the water is given easy entry directly to the house. If you have any hesitation about clambering onto the roof to see any signs of advanced deterioration in a box gutter, you should seek the advice of a roofing contractor. The care and maintenance of box gutters is such that many older homes have had them removed over the years and replaced with attached, exterior gutters.

In the case of all gutters, look for an accumulation of leaves and sticks and other debris. This buildup can lead to damming or overflow from the gutters or downspouts, defeating their purpose.

ASSESSMENT OF CHECKPOINT NO. 4

MISCELLANEOUS CONCERNS: Since the biggest single investment your roof is likely to require of you is a new surface, the key determination at this checkpoint is whether the present surface is in good condition. Are the joints between the planes of the roof and between the roof and any projection tightly sealed? If your answer to both questions is an emphatic yes, the roof has passed the most critical tests.

IMMEDIATE IMPROVEMENT INDEX: All of the following problems demand immediate attention, but they also require that you climb onto the roof to do the work. The same concerns apply to working on the roof that did to inspecting it: don't do it if you are not confident of your balance or if you do not have the proper ladders and scaffolding.

I — The need for minor repairs of the flashing in one or two areas;

— Indications that small repairs are required on the gutters or downspouts.

II — Signs that ice dams occur and that extensive flashing or electrical cables need to be installed;

— Indications that the chimney needs repointing or needs to be lined;

— The need for considerable repair or replacement of gutters and downspouts;

— Absence of a drip cap on the chimney;

— The need for repairs of flashing in a number of areas.

III — The need to resurface the roof: cupping or curling of more than a quarter of the cedar or asphalt shingles in any portion of the roof; numerous missing or broken slates or tiles; numerous broken or cracked asbestos shingles; tears or bubbles in a flat roof;

— A flat roof without ventilation or runoffs is almost sure to develop problems, sooner or later; you should get an expert appraisal of both the prevention (if there is still time) and the cure;

— Box gutters that are badly deteriorated and need reconstruction.

WALK-AWAY FACTORS: Noticeable dips or sags in the roofline indicate structural weakness; when coupled with a need for resurfacing the roof, a sagging roof is a Walk-Away Factor. Even if the roof surface appears to be in good condition, be sure to follow up any sagging carefully in the attic: good reasons may be found there to walk away as well.

THE GARAGE AND OTHER OUTBUILDINGS

An attractive, well-designed, and sturdily constructed garage adds value to a home; one that is in disrepair, that is unsightly or out of sync with the design of the house may be nothing more than a liability.

If you have an automobile aficionado in your family, this may become a home-within-the-home, so be sure you take that person with you for this stop on the tour. One customer of ours has had us inspect several houses for her, only to have her husband veto the purchase on the basis of what he regarded as unsatisfactory garage facilities.

If there is a garage, is it attached to the house or not? It is a matter of personal taste as to which is preferable: in cold climates, it is convenient to be able to walk directly from the car to the house, but some people find it more visually appealing to have the garage separate—and a good deal distant—from the house. This distinction, along with questions of color, whether the needs of your three-car family are satisfactorily served by a two-stall garage, and the other personal issues, are up to you.

One good way to address these questions is to compare the garage at your present house to the one at the house you are inspecting. Does it offer you the same space for storage? Are you going to lose space for your tools and the children's inflatable beach toys? You know best what your needs and expectations are, so compare them to the new garage.

If there is no garage and you want one, is there space on the property for one? Be sure that you check the zoning regulations in your area, too, as many communities specify set-back distances from roads and property boundaries that may affect your building plans.

THE EXTERIOR

Begin by inspecting the walls and roof of the structure just as you did the house, looking for signs of deterioration on the siding, leaks or advanced wear in the roof, for problems in the basic structure—like sagging and settling. Look for water damage and decay, using your screwdriver on the lower regions to probe for softness. Check the flashing on the roof and caulking around doors and windows.

Where is the garage located in the yard? Is it convenient to the house?

After completing your exterior inspection, approach the building from the garage door side. Open and close the door several times. If the door mechanism is motorized, make sure that it works properly: there should be no grinding noises or any changes in the rate at which the door opens and closes. Those could be signals of trouble to come. The single most expensive repair to be made inside a garage usually involves the door. You may want to take on garage door problems if you are an experienced Handyman, but the spring devices, complexity, and sheer weight of a typical door suggest that the Rookie and Apprentice leave it to the experts.

Is the door light enough for all the members of your family to handle? Does it close tightly, or is there a gap at the foot that could allow animals and the elements to enter? Are there gaps between the door sections? If the garage is attached to the house, such unneeded ventilation can lead to substantial energy loss. Does the door lock?

Does the driveway slope toward the garage? If so, you should check particularly carefully at the base of the door and the frame around it for signs of water and termite damage.

THE INTERIOR

If the garage is attached to the house, begin by looking at the wall that adjoins the house. It should be covered with a fireproof material like plaster or stucco or wallboard of 5/8" thickness. This is required by most fire codes, so that the surface will act as a fire wall in the event of a garage fire, limiting its spread.

The door leading immediately to the house should also be sheet-metal clad or of other fireproof construction. The door sill should be above the level of the garage floor, and most fire codes require that it open into the garage.

Whether or not it is attached to the house, does it fulfill your needs? For one thing, make sure it's big enough. One owner-built home we know of in Massachusetts was constructed in the days of the Model T, and the garage is big enough for a Tin Lizzie—but not for one of today's full-sized cars. So if the garage looks small to you, measure it.

Look around carefully: Are there any signs of water damage on the walls or ceiling? Don't forget to look at the ceiling over the door if the door is the overhead type, one that travels on a track over the bay of the garage.

What is the floor made of? If the house is quite old, it may be wood, and a structural engineer or architect should be consulted if you have any doubt about the floor being able to bear the weight of your automobile. If it is dirt, your inspection of the base of the walls is all the more important, and you should mark it on your Checksheet so that you return here when you are inspecting the foundation of the house, at Checkpoints 6 and 7.

If the floor is concrete, check for a drain. Make sure it works: pour a coffee can of water into it. Is the floor intact, or are there cracks or heaves? Are there stains or other indications of oil spills on the floor?

Is the lighting adequate? Is it accessible to the driver of the car who returns at night, or must an obstacle course be traveled to reach the switch? Is there an electrical receptacle for the power tools you use to clean your car or garage, or to provide for your needs if there is room for a workbench? There should be at least one outlet.

Note on your Checksheet if the hot water heater, furnace, or main electrical panel (fuse box) is located in the garage to be sure you come back there at Checkpoints 8 and 9.

OUTBUILDINGS

If there are any outbuildings, try to determine what they were originally intended for. This is particularly important if they were chicken houses or barns, as the prolonged presence of animal waste frequently leads to serious decay and other damage to the floorboards and structural members.

Inspect the exterior as you did that of the main house and garage. Are the siding and roofing materials in good condition? Is the roofline straight? Are there broken windows? Is the building a danger to the neighbor's children or to yours?

Check the interior as you did the garage: Is there electricity there? Check carefully for animal signs, not only of the domestic kind but for rodent and bird-life, too.

What use would you put the building to? Is the ceiling tall enough to accommodate you and whatever things you will be storing? Are there adequate entrances and exits? Are there windows or louvers for ventilation? Is there a heat source and any insulation if you intend to use it during the winter and you live in a cool or cold climate?

ASSESSMENT OF CHECKPOINT NO. 5

MISCELLANEOUS CONCERNS: As with the garage, outbuildings can make a house more valuable and more practical: an extra structure can be converted to an office or studio and may make a house that isn't quite big enough for your needs fit the bill with a little expenditure of energy and building materials. But make sure you know what you have and don't have. Come back to this checkpoint later if you are counting on using any outbuildings; the discussions ahead of termites and foundations will have an important bearing on your determinations here.

IMMEDIATE IMPROVEMENT INDEX: If you find any of the following problems, you should try to solve them as soon as possible:

I — The garage or other outbuilding needs a paint job.

II — The garage needs some minor repairs to the roof or siding;

— The garage door needs replacement;

— The garage or outbuilding has no electricity and a line must be run from the house.

III — The garage needs an entirely new roof surface; it must be re-sided; the foundation shows signs of serious decay and will have to have major attention.

WALK-AWAY FACTORS: The garage and outbuildings being so peripheral to the house, there are no obvious Walk-Away Factors at this checkpoint. However, if you are buying the property with the expectation that one or several of the buildings in addition to the house will be used, make sure they meet your needs.

On the other hand, if you are buying an old farm and there are several dilapidated old buildings that you have no intention of rehabilitating, consider the fact that it is expensive to have buildings torn down and if they are dangerous to visitors—invited or otherwise—the community may compel you to take the buildings down. Thus, the possibility of spending numerous thousands of dollars in demolition costs may constitute a Walk-Away Factor for some properties.

Part II

HIDDEN AND MECHANICAL AREAS

Checkpoint No. 6

THE FOUNDATION

The foundation of the house is among the most critical stops on your inspection tour. Besides assessing the overall soundness of the structure in the load-bearing areas in the basement, you can more readily determine the existence of water problems, dry rot, uneven settlement, and other maladies when you are "down under."

Begin your inspection of the foundation by walking around its perimeter, inside and outside, looking for signs of deterioration. Open all doors and windows in the basement, and don't skip closets or any rooms partitioned off in the cellar. Generally you are looking for signs of cracking, dampness, and decay. Are there any odors? Are there animal signs (i.e. animal feces)? Does the place feel damp?

Except in very old houses where fieldstone or brick has been used, the foundation material will be either poured concrete, cinder block, or concrete block. The walls are built on top of footings buried in the earth. Although it is more common in commercial buildings than in residential construction, solid, poured concrete is stronger and less prone to cracking and leakage than the blocks; of the blocks, concrete is stronger than cinders. Be aware that often blocks are covered with a skin coat of cement so poured concrete can be confused with blocks camouflaged with the thick layer of concrete. A poured concrete foundation will usually reveal itself by the pattern of the form, or mold, into which the liquid was poured: when the form is removed, an imprint of its seams and variations is left on the wall.

The age of the house is important. If the house is less than ten years old, soil and settlement problems may well not have manifested themselves. Variables like soil that shrinks or expands may have an enormous impact on a foundation, causing it to crack: if the house is less than ten years old, call the local office of your state's geological or housing administration and inquire about the soils in the area: Are settlement problems commonplace?

SLABS, CRAWL SPACES, AND BASEMENTS

Most houses in the United States are built either on a concrete slab or on top of a crawl space or basement. A slab is exactly what it sounds like, a thick strip of concrete. The house is built directly on top of the concrete, so there is no space beneath it to inspect. Since, like an iceberg, only a small portion of the slab will be visible, you will have to be very observant when inspecting the floors and walls on the ground floor for signs of water damage.

A crawl space foundation usually has a very low ceiling, typically ranging from one and a half to three feet high. You will probably have to get down on all fours to make your way across it. However, do not avoid examining the foundation simply because it is difficult. A crawl space will often reveal many of the same danger signs a full basement will, only more so since there is a smaller volume of air (and usually less ventilation) to dissipate the moisture. A flashlight and proper clothing (the floors are usually dirt) will help you make a thorough and quick examination.

How deep are the concrete footings set? In areas where frost is never a problem, footings should be at least a foot deep. Houses have been known to be shifted all out of level by frost heaves, particularly when the foundation is a crawl space inadequately footed in the earth. In the north where frost can do this sort of violent harm, each footing should be buried at least three and one half feet deep. Six inches below the frost line is the minimum.

In the case of a full basement or crawl space, the depth of the footing is the distance from the ground level outside to the floor of the basement or crawl space, plus whatever portions cannot be seen. In the case of slabs and piered basements (see the next section), it can be difficult to discern the depth of the footing, short of excavation, so your inspection of the floors and walls upstairs and their levelness and plumb is all the more important. If everything is square and there are no cracks or other signs of uneven settlement (and the house is at least five years old), the house passes this test.

PIERS OR POSTS

Where the water table is especially high or the terrain sandy, a house may be constructed on posts or piers. When properly maintained, such foundations give good service, but check a post-and-pier foundation just as you would a crawl space or basement. Are the footings themselves sound? Are there indications of movement around them?

Is the ground around them eroded, or are the beams they support out of level?

If there is any sign of water in the basement and the posts are wood, were they treated with creosote (a wood preservative, dark brown in color, with a distinct odor not unlike that of turpentine) or pressure-treated (a slightly green cast suggests pressure treating)? If they were not treated, you should check very carefully for decay using your screwdriver as a probe.

Do the posts rest on the concrete footings? No portion of them can be submerged in the footing, otherwise decay is virtually guaranteed. Refer back to Checkpoint 3, as this variety of foundation is essentially the same as that discussed in inspecting the deck.

CRACKING AND SHIFTING

Regardless of the kind of foundation you are inspecting, your first concern should be to look for signs of movement. A little settling is inevitable, but outward signs of recent movement that are discernible to the naked eye are matters for concern. If you noted in your exterior inspection that the house appeared to be out of square or that the eave lines angled, check the basement walls for uneven settlement.

As you did outside, eye the length of the wall standing at one end, as close to the wall as possible, and squint toward the other end. Does it bulge? Is it vertical, or does it tip at the top or bottom? Does the footing beneath appear to have shifted?

A cracking or shifting problem in only one section of the foundation can be cured at reasonable cost, but it may be symptomatic of something more serious, especially if the house is less than five years old. However, correcting the problem is likely to involve excavation and jacking, so it is likely to be beyond the skills of all but the most experienced Handyman. If you find serious cracks or signs of settling, you should at least consult a professional home inspector or a contractor; serious problems of this kind can be a Walk-Away Factor.

Look for cracking. Vertical cracks usually suggest that the base, or "footing," on which the foundation rests is probably insufficient. A crack in a stairlike pattern (following the outlines of concrete or cinder blocks) usually indicates a very weak foundation. Small cracks are not unusual, but unfortunately only by observing them over a period of several months can you establish whether the crack is growing worse and why. Once again, the age of the house is your best guide: even small cracks are worrisome in a new house (less than five years old) while in an older home those same small cracks (no more than a foot or two long, no wider than a quarter of an inch, in only one limited area) are not surprising.

Don't forget the floor. Check it, too, for cracks. Tap it here and there with your hammer. A hollow sound suggests that the floor may not be thick enough, or that there's space underneath into which water could seep and make your basement constantly damp. We've seen one house that was built on top of a spring: the basement was wet year-round, and the owners found that their dollars and their labors could only alleviate the wetness, not eliminate it. The floor inspection might well tell you of such a problem. However, the age of the house again comes into consideration: in a home that has been in place a number of years, that hollow sound is probably nothing to worry about if there are no other indications of weakness or wetness in the cellar.

CHIMNEY FOUNDATION

If there is a chimney (or chimneys) in the home, the foundation beneath will be visible in the cellar or crawl space. Inspect it as you have the rest of the foundation and as you would a masonry wall. If you noted a pronounced tilt to the chimney on your exterior inspection, look for further indications in the footing. Is there any evidence of uneven settlement, like cracks? Does the chimney stand straight and strong?

Is there any deterioration of the bricks or mortar? One difference from the other masonry in the home is that chimney and fireplace applications are subject to a buildup of creosote, a dark sticky by-product of wood burning. Are there any signs of creosote seeping out from between the bricks? If so, you should have a trained chimney sweep clean and inspect your fireplaces and chimneys before using them, as there is likely to be a problem with the flue. Note the signs of seeping creosote on your Checklist for follow-up at Checkpoint 13.

In an older home, particularly one built in the nineteenth century, look for lumber between the rows of brick in the piers supporting the chimney and fireplaces. Check it for decay: Visually, is it symmetrical, or have portions crumbled? Use your rot tester, the screwdriver. It was common practice in those days to incorporate wood; unfortunately, if the basement is allowed to remain wet for any length of time, that wood is as subject to decay as any other, which can cause serious settlement problems for fireplaces and chimneys.

Is there any wood in contact with the chimney? Wood and other flammable materials must be at least two inches away from the chimney: in the event of a chimney fire, the flames will lick through any gap in the lining of the stack and may ignite nearby combustibles.

DAMPNESS

Except in very arid climates, a little basement dampness is to be expected. What you are looking for is evidence of wetness in the form of puddles or serious water stains on the walls. There are other signs as well, so look carefully: in one especially damp basement we inspected during the winter, tiny ice crystals that looked like sparkles were all over the beams and floor joists. Needless to say, the decay in that basement was advanced.

If in Checkpoint 1 you noticed that the yard pitched toward the house on any side, or at Checkpoint 4 that a downspout seemed to drain too close to the house, examine that section of the basement closely. Sometimes this sort of poor drainage can create virtual babbling brooks in a basement. If your inspection leaves you unsure, try to arrange for another trip through the cellar a few hours after a heavy rain.

Ventilation is crucial to minimizing moisture in a basement. Are there windows or vents that can be opened? Without adequate ventilation, even a small amount of dampness can cause considerable damage.

Perhaps the most obvious water sign of all is a sump pump. Look for a pump whose business end disappears into the floor. Remember, a sump pump isn't installed as a preventive measure. If there are objects such as cardboard boxes stored on the floor, check them for water stains. If you find none and there is a considerable volume of goods stored downstairs, it seems likely the basement is generally dry.

The inspection process is made slightly more difficult

if the walls and floors of a basement are finished. If the walls appear to have been recently painted, look carefully for discoloration or other signs, as the paint may well have been put there to hide water stains. Look for water signs near the floor in particular. Wall-to-wall carpeting that has been wet often will have shrunk: check to see if the carpeting is flush to the walls.

If the foundation is a crawl space, look for a thick sheet of polyethylene (a "vapor barrier") on the bare ground. It is designed to keep any ground moisture on the underside of the plastic, away from the wood and the house. Even a Rookie can (and should) add one if it isn't there, but its absence suggests your search for decay should be all the more diligent.

DECAY

As we discussed earlier, no wood that has been dry throughout its life ever got dry rot. On the other hand, damp wood usually develops a microscopic, parasitic growth of fungi. An early sign of too much moisture in or on the wood is often abnormal color—sometimes a brownish tinge quite different from the rest of the wood you see in the basement, other times a bleached, whitish tone. There is also a loss of sheen to the wood. Often a single beam will, within a few inches, reveal both brownish decay and healthier wood.

If the decay is very advanced, the wood will show signs of checking, a disintegration into tiny cubes. Fine black lines within an otherwise bleached appearance or strandlike fungal growths also indicate serious decay. We have seen cases where the wood was so rotten that, literally, a child could squeeze a two-inch by four-inch piece of lumber between his thumb and forefinger.

Decay most often starts in the wood nearest the foundation. First check the sills, which are the lowest members of the frame of the house and rest horizontally on the foundation. Next check the joists, which run across the ceiling of the cellar. They are the parallel beams that, most often, are approximately two inches thick and six to twelve inches high. They support the floor above. Check the beams that support the joists, too, for rot and softness.

If you are not an experienced woodworker, compare the resistance of the wood in the basement or crawl space to that of a piece of wood you know to be sound. Remember, any sign of insects is an important danger signal (see Checkpoint 7). If the screwdriver easily enters the wood, pry it up or down rather than drawing it straight out. Dry wood cracks as it breaks, rotten wood quietly gives way or crumbles.

Rarely does decay occur to a single beam or member; usually it is an area that sustains damage. Replacement or shoring up of decayed beams and joists may be within the skills of a Handyman, but evidence of considerable decay is also a Walk-Away Factor.

ASSESSMENT OF CHECKPOINT NO. 6

MISCELLANEOUS CONCERNS: What plans do you have for the basement areas? Don't plan on putting in a playroom if you found numerous signs of water entering. Will the basement be useful for storage? Is it accessible, or is there only one narrow staircase for you to take Grandfather's steamer trunk down? Is there access from the outside, too? Are there fittings for a washer and dryer? Is the cellar secure, from animals and humans, as well as water?

IMMEDIATE IMPROVEMENT INDEX: The following problems demand your immediate attention:

I — The need for a vapor barrier in a crawl space.

II — The absence of adequate ventilation in a basement or crawl space, requiring the installation of louvers or windows;

— Water stains and other signs that the basement is chronically damp but with no accompanying decay in the wood structure of the house;

— Posts in a pier-and-post foundation whose lower ends are immersed in the concrete footings;

— A chimney foundation that is evidently weakened: the chimney or its footing is evidently askew; wood members built into its support are badly decayed.

III — The presence of decay in a confined area of the basement;

— Evidence of uneven settlement on only one wall or a small section of a house that is more than five years old.

WALK-AWAY FACTORS: Numerous cracks or other signs of uneven settlement of the foundation constitute a Walk-Away Factor: if the foundation of the house is settling into the earth in such a way that it is being pulled and pushed, the structure of the house above is also subject to such stresses and strains. It may take years, but eventually the damage to the house will be substantial—and expensive to correct.

Another Walk-Away Factor is extensive decay in the sills, joists, or beams. If your screwdriver routinely plunges deep into the members that support the house, walk away. Replacing or boxing-in the old, decayed wood is expensive and, as often as not, the problems you see are only the beginning. Few contractors will give you a final estimate of the costs to repair such problems before beginning the job, and when the work is under way some sorry surprises are almost inevitably found.

It is at this checkpoint that the most dangerous structural problems are to be found. If you found no serious trouble "down under," then you have made a major stride in establishing the structural integrity of the building.

TERMITES AND
OTHER INSECTS

The mere mention of termites inspires fear in the average homeowner. Ironically, termites and carpenter ants are social insects: they organize themselves into colonies, with a division of labor, complete with queens and workers and soldiers. But the product of their labors certainly doesn't qualify as sociable behavior, at least by human standards.

Damp, dark environments are their favorites, and in the forest they find congenial homes in dead trees that have fallen to the ground. In the wild, they help maintain nature's balance, living on cellulose, the organic substance of which wood is composed, and in doing so help clear away the old dead growth to make room for the new. In and near houses, they most often establish their settlements in chunks of lumber or stumps buried by the builder in the ground outside the home. And it is from such outposts that they may have launched their assault on the structure of your home.

SUBTERRANEAN TERMITES

Subterranean termites are like suburban businessmen: they commute from their homes to their places of work. Termites live in the earth outside a house, and travel via tunnels of their own construction to their work site inside.

Termites avoid the rays of the sun. In the process, they also evade detection by all but the most careful and experienced human eye. They prefer boring their way along the grain at the heart of a piece of wood to clambering like a spider over its surface. More often than not, termites are discovered after they have spent years inside the timber of a house.

If you found any wood that was flush to the ground (or closer than five inches from the soil) at Checkpoint 2, get as close as you can inside the basement or crawl space to that portion of the house. Do the same if your inspection of the garage or deck or porch areas revealed any lumber close to or in contact with the ground.

Probe the wood with your screwdriver, inside and outside the foundation. Again, try to do it in the least obvious, lowest areas. You're more likely to find insects and less likely to raise the seller's ire. (If your house was constructed on a slab, your exterior inspection will have to be all the more careful because you cannot follow up in the basement. If, however, there are any lower portions of the house that can be reached through access doors, through closet floors, or by other means, check there as well.)

Some sidings (like cedar and redwood) are more resistant to insects than others, but probe them too. Check the timber closest to the ground and, inside the basement, probe the sills (the timbers that rest on top of the foundation wall) and the first foot or more of any wood members (beams and joists) that extend away from the external walls toward the center of the house.

If there is a heavy termite infestation, your screwdriver will slide into the heart of the board when you stab it. Inside, you will uncover channels the termites have eaten in the wood. These so-called galleries run parallel to the grain since the termite likes the softer portions of the wood and avoids the denser wood that is the product of summer growth. Inside the galleries you will find gray signs of the termites, a residue of earth and excrement.

If you find minute quantities of sawdust on the floor or on any horizontal surface beneath the beams and joists, you probably have carpenter ants; if the galleries appeared smooth, almost polished, that, too, indicates carpenter ants (see page 77). On the other hand, if you find "shelter tubes"—strawlike structures made of mud—along the foundation or plumbing pipes or even free standing, they are clear indications of a termite presence. If when you break into one there is no sign of the insects, that doesn't mean the problem has cured itself, as they may be using other tubes to reach preferred feeding grounds.

If there are any cracks in the masonry foundation, check there, too, for tubes, as the termites will use any means of entry to the house. Did you notice any tubes behind the vines or shrubs outside?

Make sure you check any and all wood that is in immediate contact with the earth, including posts on the dirt floor inside the cellar, wooden staircases, and garage door frames.

DRY-WOOD TERMITES

The termites we have just discussed are subterranean termites. There is another variety as well, one commonly found in the South and Southwest.

Dry-wood termites are not commuters; they are likely both to live and work in an attic. They are substantially less numerous than their in-the-ground cousins, but are also social insects. And they, too, prefer to attend to their labors inside of the wood on which they dine.

The key piece of evidence to look for is the presence of small pellets. They are left behind by the termites, and may tumble out from cracks in the wood. If you come across either the pellets or galleries filled with them, you should stop your probing, as the usual way to deal with them is to inject the galleries with an insecticide, and for this to be effective, the galleries should be intact.

CARPENTER ANTS,
POWDER-POST BEETLES

As we have noted, signs of sawdust indicate carpenter ants, as do polished or shiny galleries. Though both insects have wings, the carpenter ants themselves look quite different from termites: the black ants have segmented bodies, with an evident hourglass shape. Termites are pale, with a thickened waistline, making them appear more uniformly cylindrical. Carpenter ants are also larger, as big as a half inch in length.

Unlike the dry-wood termites, carpenter ants prefer moist wood. Unlike the subterranean termites, they are not commuters, but they are apt to be found wandering around the living spaces of the house. Inspecting for carpenter ants involves probing in the attic and cellar, particularly around areas where it is evident from staining that it has been damp; and, in particular, keeping a wary eye out for large ants in the house itself.

Another insect to be on the lookout for is the powder-post beetle. The most likely indication of powder-post beetles are their tiny, round exit holes in wood members of the house. Powder-post beetles are a less serious problem, as they normally infest only the surface of beams. Active powder-post beetles leave little piles of sawdust on a cellar floor, or at the entrance to their holes bored in the wood. Look for their activity by examining cobwebs that catch the sawdust. This will be a bright yellowish brown if fresh, gray if aged.

ASSESSMENT OF CHECKPOINT NO. 7

MISCELLANEOUS CONCERNS: Many banks and some states require a termite inspection (most often at the seller's expense) before closing. Make sure one is done if it is required, and it is a good idea even if it is not. Provide the inspector with your observations, as well, if you think you have uncovered signs of termite or other insect damage, and be sure to discuss with him what he found at the sites that worried you.

IMMEDIATE IMPROVEMENT INDEX: The following problems demand your immediate attention:

I — A minor infestation of insects that requires a visit (or two) by an exterminator but no reconstruction.

II — A more serious infestation in which enough damage has been done in one discrete portion of the house that some carpentry and other work is required to undo the damage the insects have done.

III — A major, long-term assault by termites or other insects is discovered, in which some structural members are involved.

WALK-AWAY FACTORS: The presence of insects in a home often provokes a strong, instinctive reaction, that is, to run, not walk, away from the property.

The fact is that even a large community of termites or other insects probably has not seriously damaged a significant portion of the structure. A professional should certainly be consulted; not even the Handyman should be tempted to a self-diagnosis if signs are uncovered of recent insect damage, particularly since the seller will probably have to foot the inspector's bill.

With the results of the termite inspector's examination in hand, a contractor can be called in to estimate the costs of correcting the damage. If the damage is only superficial, an Apprentice may be able to take on the job; if there is only minor structural work, the Handyman may be up to the task.

Rarely is a termite infestation a death knell for the structure of a house. A large swarm of some hundred thousand termites will consume less than a single, eight-foot length of a two-by-four in a year; given that a typical partition between rooms consists of a dozen or more lengths of two-by-four lumber and a whole house of many hundreds, clearly the damage the swarm can do even over a period of years is finite.

Further, once the termite infestation has been discovered, it can be treated and stopped. Inspections should be made annually in the South and the Southwest, every other year elsewhere after a termite infestation has been uncovered and treated, but this is as a precaution, as some insecticides can protect a house for a quarter century. So if you find a problem, get the seller to agree to correct it before closing; but don't walk away from your dream house because of insects alone. Insect damage is likely to be a Walk-Away Factor only in instances where the bugs have had the run of the house for many years, as in the case of a house that has been abandoned.

Checkpoint No. 8

THE ELECTRICAL SYSTEM

There are still houses in this country without electricity, but the odds are high that the house you want to buy will rely upon it as the primary source of light and power.

Let's begin with a warning that's really a pep talk: you should always be wary and respectful of electricity. Electricity is a little like a bully from your childhood—you couldn't afford to be afraid of him, but there was no sense in provoking his wrath, either. The point, then, is to know your limits, to be cautious and sensible—and always to think about safety first.

You should have an electrical tester. It doesn't have to be an elaborate device that can measure amperes and volts and watts; for the most part, you will need it only to determine whether or not there is current (or "juice") in a line. To put it another way, you must be able to determine whether a line is "hot." A simple tester with a pair of wires connecting two conductors to a test bulb is all you need, and it should not cost more than two or three dollars at your local hardware store. But make sure it is a tester designed for 110- or 120-volt systems, and not a 12-volt tester for automotive applications.

Before embarking on this part of this inspection, you should memorize a couple of safety precautions.

**Never, ever, whether it is in the inspection process or in the course of your everyday affairs, associate yourself in any way with an electrical appliance or device while you are standing on a damp floor, in a puddle, or are "grounding" yourself in any way. Grounding occurs when an electrical current goes to a point of lower potential: if you are simultaneously in contact with an improperly installed or damaged electrical line or piece of equipment that as a result has "floating" voltage, and you are also in contact with a conductor (like a water pipe or a damp floor or a steel post or any other object that, rather than being an insulator—like wood or glass, for example—is a conductor), then the current will pass through you. In such circumstances, you become, in essence, a part of the ground, and you will get a shock. Little shocks are more surprising than painful, but big ones can be fatal.

**The Rookies and the Apprentices should not try to remove the cover on the fuse box or circuit breaker panel; Handymen without electrical experience should also beware. The cover is there to protect the uninitiated from "hot" wires.

One other consideration before we embark on the specifics of the inspection is that when it comes to the electricians they, like other tradesmen, have a special jargon for the constituent parts of the electrical system, for their tools, for the tasks involved in the installation and maintenance of equipment. You will probably find that when it comes to the electrical system in the home in particular it is useful to learn a few of the terms before talking with the power company or with an electrician.

When you're talking to a carpenter, it is not difficult to get your point across by adapting everyday words, by drawing sketches, or even using gestures and hand motions. But it seems that talking about electricity defies the utility of most people's everyday vocabularies. So try to remember a few of the key words, like service entrance, meter pad, panel, and ground.

THE SERVICE ENTRANCE

The so-called service entrance is the combination of components that tie the wiring in your house to the source of power in the vicinity, usually the local electric company. The main components of the service entrance are the "service drop," the "meter pad," and the "service panel."

Unless the power to the house is delivered underground, you will see two or three large wires that link the house with the nearest power lines. (Don't confuse the lighter gauge phone wires with the electrical wires.) The wires that run from the power company's pole to your home are termed the service drop. In the case of an underground entrance, the power is delivered through cables that are buried underground and are not available to the eye for inspection.

If there are only two lines, then accept as fact that the electrical power coming into the house is going to be insufficient by today's standards. With only two lines, which means there is one ground line and one "hot" line, you cannot have an air conditioner or baseboard heater or electric stove that requires 220-volt current. Houses built before 1935 that have not had their systems updated are likely to have systems that deliver a maximum of 120 volts. This rates a *III* on the Immediate Improvement Index.

Visually examine the overhead wires for any signs of deterioration: Is the insulation worn and the conductor beneath bare? Are there any branches or other interferences near enough to the wires that are already in contact with the wires or that could fall onto them? Are the wires located such that they are accessible to unknowing hands, as from the ground or an upper-story window?

Any of these situations is hazardous and requires correction. Circumstances vary from one power company to the next, but often the utility company is responsible for the maintenance of the wires to the point at which they join your house. If there are signs of worn insulation or interfering branches, call the local power company and discuss the problem with a customer service representative. But given the danger of the high-powered currents running through the service drop, you should let the experts deal with this one unless you are a licensed electrician.

The service drop ties into the meter pad. The meter pad holds a glass globe that, in turn, contains the meter that keeps track of the power used in the house. The box, or pad, into which the self-contained meter is plugged is sealed to prevent the customer from bypassing it and taking unrecorded electricity.

Generally it is from the globe that you can learn the number of amperes in your service. This piece of information is essential to determine whether the power in the house is adequate for your purposes or not. Most often houses constructed today have 100, 150, or 200 amperes of power in their services. Older homes commonly have 60, though a small number still have as few as 15 or 30.

If the meter reads 15 or 30 amps, however, that may not be the capacity of the service. In one house we in-

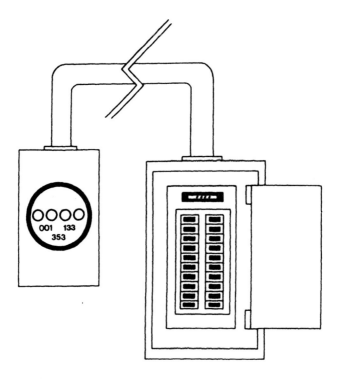

PLATE 1. The Service Entrance

The meter is inside the glass globe on the left; the service panel is the rectangular box on the right. The number of amps being delivered to your house can be determined from either the printing on the face of the meter or from the main circuit breaker at the top of the panel.

spected in upstate New York, we found an old meter that was rated at 15 amps, but checking with the power company revealed that the house actually had 60 amps—the 15 amps cited on the meter was the "test amperage." In any case, a meter with a test amperage of 15 amps is unlikely to have more than 60 amps. As we will discuss shortly, another way to check the amperage is at the breaker panel or fuse box.

Determining whether or not the house has enough electricity for your needs is relatively easy. The typical American home today has numerous appliances, including such major consumers of electricity as electric water heaters, clothes washers or dryers, central air conditioners, and cooking ranges. If you have one of these major electrical appliances and you use an average amount of power in your everyday activities around the house—that is, you have a color TV and a toaster, and somebody in your household uses an electric blow dryer for his or her hair—then 60 amperes is almost surely not enough for your needs. If you have two of the appliances we mentioned, then 150 amperes is more like what you require. If you have electric heat—or are considering its installation—then you require 200 or more amperes.

If you determine that a larger service entrance is required, you may wish to perform the installation yourself. However, all but the Handyman with some electrical experience should refrain from doing so. In addition, you should check with your power company and/or local building inspector to be sure you are allowed to do the work. In some states, only licensed electricians are permitted to install new service entrances.

THE FUSE BOX OR BREAKER PANEL

From the meter, the current is delivered to the breaker panel or fuse box. While the meter is generally outside to enable the meter reader to do his job without having to knock on your door every month, the panel is usually indoors (though in some older homes, particularly in rural areas, the panel is found outside adjacent to the meter). In homes with full basements, the panel is usually found downstairs, while attached garages are the best candidates in houses built on slabs or crawl spaces.

Homes constructed in recent years have circuit breakers rather than fuses: circuit breakers are permanent switches that are "tripped" when their circuits overload, stopping the flow of electricity to the lines. They can be switched back on and do not have to be replaced, while fuses require replacement once they have "blown."

First determine whether the panel is fused or if circuit breakers were used. A panel with circuit breakers is probably of recent vintage, most likely not more than twenty or twenty-five years old. Look at the wiring leading into the panel: Is it neatly and safely stapled to the wall, or is there extra cable that dangles like clothesline, a dangerous temptation to little or careless hands? Are there any signs of standing water in the vicinity of the box, either on the wall behind, the floor below, or the roof above the panel? The cover on the panel should be tightly affixed, and only the fuses or the circuit breakers should be visible; often there is a hinged access door that can be snapped open to get access to the breakers or fuses.

Look at the fuses or breakers. There will be a large disconnect at the top of the box, the so-called main. If it is labeled, it will tell you how large the entrance is: 60 amps, 100, or whatever. Count how many of the smaller fuses or breakers are 15-amp circuits, how many are 20. Generally appliance circuits are 20 amps, lights 15. A good rule of thumb is at least two 20-amp appliance circuits in the house, and one 15-amp light circuit for every five hundred square feet. If you find a smaller representation than that, it is likely that some of the lines are overloaded. And overloaded lines are one of the most common causes of electrical fires.

If there are fuses rather than breakers, be sure that none of the fuses has a rating greater than 15 or, at most, 20 amperes. Edison fuses (that is, those that screw into their sockets like light bulbs) come in sizes up to 30 amperes, but virtually no older house with a fused system has wires with a capacity to carry more than 15 amps.

If you find fuses for 20 and 25 or even 30 amps, you can be fairly sure the lines have been fused beyond their limit. This is a very serious fire hazard. No doubt some careless person, perhaps one who has grown tired of changing fuses every time his daughter dries her hair while he's using a power tool, has put in a fuse too large for the capacity of the line. The result is that the next time the current in the line exceeds the limit for which the wire was designed, the wire will heat up.

Ordinarily, the fuse would also heat up and when the wire (and fuse) reached their limit, the fuse would blow and the flow of electricity to the line would stop. However, with the wrong fuse in place, the wire will continue past its limit and get hotter and hotter. At a certain point, if it is in contact with any combustible material, a fire could be started. The vast majority of fires that the newspapers report as having been "electrical in origin" are caused this way.

If you find 25- or 30-amp fuses and none of the wires leaving the panel is of a dimension greater than the rest, you may be looking at an electrical system that is operating at risk. (In making this determination, be sure to ignore the very large main wires that bring the power from the meter, as it is only the smaller wires that go to the lighting and appliance circuits in the home that concern you here.)

If you buy the house, your very first act upon closing should be to buy a box of 15-amp fuses and install them. However, you would be wise to get a licensed electrician to come and have a look and give you a reading of the seriousness of the problem before you buy. The problem may be simply and inexpensively solved with the addition of a supplementary line or two, or an expensive new service entrance may be required. But at the very least, this observation indicates that the previous owner has found the capacity of the system insufficient for his needs.

Note, too, if there is a larger double circuit, perhaps of 40 amps, for an electric range. This is acceptable if there is also a noticeably heavier electrical cable leaving the box for the range. The same may be true of a hot water heater, an electric clothes dryer, or other heavy appliance.

If the cover of the box is open, look carefully inside: use your eyes and not your fingers. Is it neat? Is the insulation intact on all the wires, or has the cloth or plastic or paper worn off in places? Also, check the color of the bare wires that are connected to the contacts: are they copper or aluminum? If aluminum, you should get a licensed electrician to inspect the wiring, since aluminum wiring can be a fire hazard if it has not been installed correctly.

THE GROUND

The entire electrical system should be grounded. Electrical codes vary from state to state and even city to city, but from the meter or the panel you will see a large gauge wire that descends either to a metallic plumbing pipe or disappears into the ground itself, in which case it is clamped to a rod buried in the earth. The wire may be protected by metal armor, or it may be bare, a stranded wire that will resemble clothesline, though of coarser strands and larger in diameter.

Make a visual check to be sure the ground wire is firmly attached to its ground. Some codes require a double ground, so don't be surprised if there are two. A ground is an essential safety precaution and its absence is a serious hazard; if you cannot find the ground, expert guidance is advised.

BEWARE OF . . .

General Condition: Make a general inspection of the cables and wires that leave the panel. Follow a few of them until they disappear into the floor or walls or ceiling. Is the insulation intact? If wires intersect at junction boxes, are the boxes covered or can you see the wires inside? Covers are available at most hardware stores and can—and should be—installed on all boxes. An Apprentice can take this one on, as there should be no reason to touch any of the wires.

Are the wires tightly fastened to the surface along which they travel, or will they tempt young hands as a test of strength for a tug or two? Are there any exposed wires or connections?

Insulation: Check the wires that leave the panel. If the wires are covered with a metal sheathing, then the cable is called BX, which is often found in older homes and in communities where fire regulations are very stringent. In any case, it is the insulation immediately around the wire itself that is of major importance: Is the insulation cloth or plastic? If it's cloth, it is probably a little older than if it were plastic, but that isn't necessarily worse. Roll the wire gently between your thumb and fingers: if it is cloth, and at a touch the insulation begins to disintegrate, you may have worries in the future, particularly in situations where the older wiring will have to be worked, such as when you replace an old plug receptacle. If the insulation is plastic, has it grown brittle with age?

Knob-and-Tube Wiring: A now outmoded method of wiring found in homes wired early in the century is called knob-and-tube. It is not used inside of walls, so if it is to be found, you will see it running along exposed members in the basement or attic or other unfinished spaces. It is composed of porcelain insulating tubes and knobs, with wires strung through and between them. This wiring is unacceptable, particularly as it is likely to be many years old, and must be replaced.

PLUGS, LIGHTS, AND OTHER BUILT-IN ELECTRICAL UNITS

This portion of the electrical checkpoint should be followed up at later stops on the inspection, particularly in Checkpoints 15 and 17.

Begin by using your testers on every electrical outlet you see: Do they work? You should turn on and off every light in the house.

Are the outlets old-fashioned two-slot receptacles, or are they the newer, grounded variety that will accommodate three-pronged plugs? A properly wired two-slot system will accept a three-pronged plug with an adapter, but the wire on the adapter must be fixed to the screw on the plate cover to assure that the electrical device is safely grounded.

To test to be sure the outlet is properly grounded, hold one of the contacts of your tester to the screw on the cover. Then insert the other tester probe into the first, then the other plug slot. One or the other insertion should produce a glow from the test lamp. If not, then either the receptacle is not properly grounded or the plug is dead (test it to make sure it is not). If the screw on the plate cover is painted, however, you may have to loosen it a few turns to get contact with an unpainted (and, therefore, uninsulated) portion of it.

Keep an eye out for extension cords: their presence suggests inadequate electrical outlets. Look for blackened faces on electrical plugs. This suggests short circuits.

As you go through the house, recall your own appliance needs. If you plan to put a window air conditioner in every room, make sure there are plugs available for them, and remember that you must have the power as well. A rule of thumb is a 20-amp appliance circuit for each unit. If you have a computer, variations in the current may cause it to "crash," so if the service borders on inadequate, you may have a problem.

If there are built-in heaters or fans or other appliances, turn them on and off to be sure they work properly.

Note that most doorbell and thermostat wiring is only 12 or 24 volts; your tester is unlikely to give you any reading from some low voltage (and smaller diameter) lines.

ASSESSMENT OF CHECKPOINT NO. 8

MISCELLANEOUS CONCERNS: Electrical problems are one of the primary sources of house fires, so for you and your family's safety, have you determined that the wiring is in good repair and that the fusing is appropriate? Is the system properly grounded?

As for comfort and convenience, will the system fulfill your needs?

IMMEDIATE IMPROVEMENT INDEX: These problems require your immediate attention:

I — Worn insulation or interfering branches at the service drop;

— Dampness or standing water in the immediate area of the electrical panel; either the flow of water to the area should be staunched or a dry platform constructed for safer access to the panel;

— The absence of a proper ground for the electrical system;

— One or two outlets or light fixtures that need to be fixed or replaced.

II — Indications of unsafe fusing (e.g., fuses of greater than 20-amp rating in an older home with no signs of new wiring);

— Indications of outmoded wiring in the house that will have to be replaced, including knob-and-tube wiring or badly worn cloth-insulated wiring.

III — Insufficient amperage in your service entrance or electrical panel to serve your electrical needs; thus, you will need to increase the size of your service entrance;

— Only two wires in the service drop to the house, meaning an absence of 220-volt power; while it is not essential from a safety standpoint that you install a three-wire system, the chances are that your appliance needs will, sooner or later, compel you to do so.

WALK-AWAY FACTORS: The only single problem large enough to constitute a Walk-Away Factor is evidence that the house as a whole has been inadequately, carelessly, or dangerously wired. This evidence would include frequent signs of sloppy workmanship like wires hanging from ceilings or plugs or fixtures whose wiring is open to the eye and touch; badly worn insulation; insufficient grounding; or dangerously high fusing. Each of these individually, but in particular several in combination, suggest it may be best to walk away.

This is one checkpoint where, if you detect problems or you lack confidence about your determinations, you may wish to follow up with an expert, preferably a licensed electrician. Virtually any problem can be cured, but at a monetary cost that may be difficult to calculate, particularly if the corrective surgery involves cutting into finished surfaces inside the living portions of the home that will then have to be refinished or repainted or replastered. You may find that in your community you must hire an expert to do the electrical work anyway, so if you find safety concerns, check with the local building inspector regarding where to go for professional advice.

Checkpoint No. 9

HEATING AND
AIR-CONDITIONING

Most homeowners discover early on that with exception of the monthly mortgage payment, their single largest home-related expense is temperature control, either heating or cooling. Unless you make no attempt to control the environment of your home, or your house is of a very efficient solar design, odds are you will have a substantial energy cost to contend with.

We will be concerned in the following pages with trying to anticipate whether there will be expensive repairs: in fact, signs that the system needs major upgrading or repairs is a Walk-Away Factor. Even if the heating system appears in excellent condition, however, you should try to determine what the heating and cooling fuel bills will be. Don't hesitate to ask the seller for his heating bills and maintenance records.

At this checkpoint we will assess the safety and condition of the different kinds of heating and cooling systems commonly found in residential structures. But given the variations in fuel prices from one section of the country to another, it is impossible to assess accurately here the relative cost-efficiency of each system. At the same time, each kind of heating has its own advantages and disadvantages; some are inexpensive to run but not very clean, others very efficient but expensive to run.

Most homes today have central heating, that is, a furnace or boiler (the "burner") that generates the heat. In turn, the heat is delivered to the rest of the house through some sort of distribution system, most often pipes or ducts that lead to radiators or vents. There are area systems (the classic potbellied stove is a familiar example) still in use, but the bulk of this checkpoint will be devoted to the electric, gas, and oil central systems.

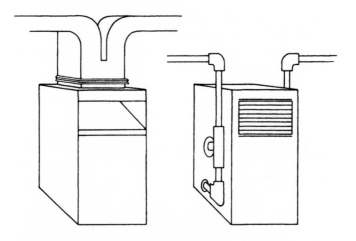

PLATE 2. The Furnace and the Boiler

A furnace heats with hot air, a boiler heats with hot water. At the left, the furnace is distinguishable because of the large ducts that extend up and away from the furnace. On the right, the pipes are part of the delivery system that takes the water or steam to the radiators above. Note the presence (or absence) of a fan or pump to force the heated air or water upward.

FURNACE VS. BOILER

Although the term is often misapplied, a furnace is a heater that produces hot air, while a boiler generates hot water. The simplest way to distinguish one from the other is the presence of pipes or ducts. While you may come across mixed breeds, generally a network of ducts, either round or square, most often at least six inches across, means the system is hot air; one-to-three-inch diameter pipes means hot water or steam. (Be careful here, though, and do not confuse the plumbing pipes with heat pipes; the former are usually smaller in size and number and are limited to the areas around the kitchen and bathrooms, while the heat pipes should go to the outside walls of virtually every room in the house.)

Whether your system involves hot water or hot air, you should begin your inspection by making sure there is no flammable material in the immediate vicinity of the furnace or boiler. The ceiling above and walls nearby should be covered with a fireproof surface that meets the local fire codes. There should be no exposed wood joists or posts or beams; if there are any, they should be protected with gypsum board or some other fireproof surface. An Apprentice or Handyman should have no trouble with this fix.

Check for ventilation. If there is a separate room for the furnace, make sure that the vents to the space have an area of an absolute minimum of one square foot (that is, one vent 12″ × 12″, four of 6″ × 6″, etc.). The vent may allow the air to enter from either outdoors or another portion of the building, but air flow is essential to provide the flame with oxygen and to minimize the accumulation of any gases or fumes that are by-products of the process. If there is no vent, the installation of one is a relatively easy task: a simple hole in the wall will provide ventilation, although the neat installation of a grille purchased at a local hardware or building supply store will be more attractive, particularly if any of the basement area is finished.

HOT AIR SYSTEMS

There are two basic categories of hot air systems: gravity and forced air. Gravity systems are rarely installed these days because they are less efficient, but they are still frequently found in older homes.

The operative principle in a gravity system is that hot air rises. If you heat air in the basement and provide it a network of paths to follow its natural inclination to rise, you'll heat your house. Many gravity systems look suspiciously like giant barrels with inverted octopuses attached to their tops. In fact, the sight is actually of a self-contained furnace beneath a network of ducts. Linking the top of the furnace to the ducts is the plenum, which distributes the furnace's heated air to the ducts.

The forced air system employs one or more fans that "force" the warm air up into the house. Forced air systems tend to look less like refugees from Rube Goldberg's imagination, as they are more compact and modern-looking. From an efficiency standpoint, the gravity systems are dinosaurs, as it takes more heat to warm the home when it must rely on the laws of nature to get the heat to the cold rooms, and the air circulation is likely to be less. But it must be said on their behalf that gravity systems oftentimes were built the way things were supposed to be built in the past: to last forever. We've seen more than a few gravity furnaces that, though they looked like Jules Verne designed them, were still doing their jobs almost half a century after installation.

To determine whether your hot air system is gravity or forced air, look for a large grate or vent in the side of the furnace. That indicates that it is a gravity system: forced air systems have a return duct that delivers air from the interior of the house back to the furnace, while the gravity system, once again, relies on nature's laws to bring the humble cold air back to the basement, usually down stairways and through first-floor vents.

A gravity system can be adapted relatively easily to become a forced air system (with a consequent saving of energy). However, it is not recommended that even the Handyman take this task on. Special tools and expertise are required.

Hot air systems have certain advantages over their water-bearing brethren. Humidifiers can be installed in the plenum to control the humidity in your home; central air conditioners can also be incorporated into them to take advantage of the duct work.

Inspect the duct work carefully: Are there apparent leaks between sections of the duct where the heated air can escape? Are the ducts insulated to ensure that you are heating the spaces you want heated rather than the cellar or garage? If not, you may want to insulate them, a job that either an Apprentice or Handyman could perform with confidence. A number of kits and publications are available to guide you in this project. And there will be a resultant savings in energy dollars.

HOT WATER AND STEAM SYSTEMS

Assuming you have discovered that pipes come and go from your boiler (rather than ducts from your furnace), you have a hot water system. Here again, there are two basic kinds of heating: forced and gravity hot water. The distinction is similar to the difference between the hot air varieties, the difference being the mechanical assist added to the forced water system, in this case via a pump rather than a fan.

If you don't know whether your system is gravity or forced, look for the circulating pump. It will be mounted near the boiler, connected to the return pipe which brings the water in the system back from the radiators to the boiler in order that it can be reheated and recirculated. The circulating pump can also be distinguished because it will be powered by an electric motor—it shouldn't be confused with any of the burner parts because neither end disappears into the boiler but both remain outside tied to the plumbing.

A steam system is distinguished by the fact that, unlike the hot water systems, which are full of water, in the case of steam the system has a good deal of air in it. In fact, no water remains in the pipes when the boiler is off and the boiler itself is only three-quarters full. When the system comes on, it brings the water to a boil, at which point the steam rises to the radiators above.

A steam system is distinguished by the absence of a circulating pump and by the presence of a water level gauge on the boiler. Also, you will find that there are escape valves on each radiator in the house above. These escape valves allow the hot air to escape and the steam to rise; when the steam comes in contact with the cool radiators above, it simultaneously heats the surface of the radiator and condenses back to water which flows back to the boiler below. Steam systems are rarely used today in new construction, but many older homes and buildings have them, particularly apartment buildings.

For reasons much like those that make the forced air system preferable to gravity air, forced water is regarded as more efficient and desirable than gravity water. By circulating the water by mechanical means rather than waiting for the temperature to do the job, the system delivers its heat more quickly and evenly. However, converting an older, gravity system to forced water is relatively simple, a matter of adding a circulating pump but, once again, it is a task best left to steamfitters or other trained, licensed experts.

In the case of steam systems, conversion is usually not possible; since separate pipes do not handle the delivery and the return of the steam as is required for a mechanically circulated heating system. If you look at the radiators in a steam system, usually there is just one pipe that must handle both tasks. If, however, your steam system is of the two-pipe variety, it can be adapted much like a gravity hot water system.

Inspect the piping that brings the water to the living areas of the house. Are there any signs of rust or corrosion? Have any of the fittings begun to leak? Check the floor and other surfaces nearby.

Is there evidence of repairs having been made on the pipes? Occasionally, when a pipe is weakened with rust or mineral buildup inside, it will leak not from a fitting (that is, the piece of hardware that joins the piping) but from the pipe itself. Look for clamp seals, where a sandwich of metal plates tied together with a rubber seal and a pair of bolts may be sealing a leak. This, and other evidence of leakage like corrosion or mineral deposits or decayed or stained wood may indicate repair problems may not be far off for the older pipes in the system.

THE FURNACE/BOILER CHECK

The most expensive portion of any central heating system is likely to be the furnace or boiler, so now that we know what we're looking at we will check it out. However, if the system apparently has not been in use for a long period, if there are any signs that a fire occurred near it, if there is evidence of any kind of fuel or gas leak, or anything else that makes you suspect the soundness and safety of the system, get your fuel supplier to test it for you. If the seller assures you there was no problem during the last cold spell, however, then when you start it up, you'll be doing exactly what the furnace should do automatically upon the arrival of cold weather in the fall.

The fuel used in air or water systems can be oil, gas, electricity, or even coal or wood. Begin this part of the inspection by determining which it is: with oil, there will be a tank, though often it is buried in the ground outside. If you don't see the tank, look for a copper tube emerging from the concrete floor and leading to the burner. You may also have noticed a fill connection during your exterior inspection.

If the tank is inside, check it for leaks. In particular, handle the bottom of the tank and the fittings where the oil is piped out to the burner. If there is indication of leakage, the tank may have to be replaced. A life expectancy for such tanks is fifteen to twenty-five years.

If the fuel is gas, it probably is piped in via a municipal system. In that case, there will be a meter. If the fuel is electricity (which is infrequently used for furnace or boiler systems), there will be evident electrical fixtures linking the heater to the electrical entrance: the wires will be substantially larger than the rest of the wires feeding the house.

Find the emergency shut-off switch and the thermostat that controls the system. Both of these are, in fact, switches, but the thermostat is set to a specific temperature and, when the temperature in its vicinity falls below that figure, it turns on the system; the emergency switch is actually a master control that shuts down the entire system and is required by fire and safety codes.

It is easier to perform this part of the inspection with an assistant. Once you've found the switches, switch the master off. Then move the thermostat up to a temperature above what it is in its vicinity. Position yourself within easy sight and hearing range of the furnace or boiler—no closer than three feet—and instruct your helper to hit the switch.

Look carefully at the furnace; watch for it to light. If it doesn't immediately, be patient for a minute or two for it may have a delay built in. When it lights, listen attentively. Do you hear any untoward noises? Banging or grinding sounds, as if some moving part is being interfered with, a burning odor in the air, or flames lapping out of the firebox mean you should command your assistant to shut it down immediately.

Look inside the firebox, the area where the flame is to be seen. Are there signs of cracking or deterioration? Some soot and grime are to be expected, but a great deal of corrosion or accumulated grit on the heating element will interfere with its functioning.

With a hot air furnace, the only time it needs to be replaced is if there is a crack in it that allows the exhaust from the combustion process to escape the furnace and enter the basement. So when the furnace is lit, check the connection to the chimney and the exterior of the furnace. Is there any smoke or odor escaping into the air of the basement?

If you come across any of these problems, you would

do well to consult the fuel company that has serviced the home. They probably have not only a record of the fuel purchased but of the system's maintenance as well. They can tell you what the problems have been—and whether or not there is one now.

If your system is forced hot air, the first event should be the burners lighting; after the air in the system's immediate vicinity is warmed to roughly a hundred degrees, the fan should come on. Listen for it; it shouldn't come on before the furnace is warm, as then it would simply circulate whatever air (including cold) is in the system. If it comes on immediately, unless the temperature in the furnace is summertime hot, there may be a switching problem.

If your system is hot water, the boiler will be made of either cast iron or steel, with the iron boiler having the greater life expectancy. Today, manufacturers often give a twenty-year guarantee, but in the case of older boilers, the metal is of a heavier gauge, so it is not uncommon to find them still functioning well forty and more years later.

A boiler must be replaced only when it leaks, although you may elect to replace it for reasons of efficiency or to save space, as some of the older boilers are literally five or more times the size of today's installations. When you inspect, look carefully for signs of leakage in and immediately around the boiler. If pipes are leaking nearby, that's a much easier fix and probably has nothing whatsoever to do with the boiler. If you see any signs of water in the firebox, however, you should get an expert consultation.

If the system uses steam or forced water, there must be an automatic pressure-release valve. This is a safety for the system: in the event the pressure builds up beyond a certain point, this valve will relieve the pressure before it causes damage elsewhere in the system. The relief valve should be mounted on the boiler itself. If you do not find one—or if it is located some distance away on the feed or return lines—one should be installed on the boiler. Again, this is best left to either a Handyman with considerable plumbing experience or a professional steamfitter.

There should also be pressure and temperature gauges on forced hot water and steam systems. Their absence suggests that you should consult a professional for guidance as to what needs to be done (the system may be archaic, or badly installed) and what it will cost.

ELECTRIC HEAT

Electric baseboard heat has a number of advantages. Its initial cost is low, and it is very efficient. It is also very clean. However, depending upon the electrical rates in your area, it can be very expensive.

If the heat in the home you are inspecting is electric, look for wall-mounted thermostats. Another advantage of electrical heat is that it allows the house to be divided into zones: a number of thermostats can control the baseboard units in different sections of the house. In some cases, the controls are room by room.

WOOD STOVES AND OTHER AREA HEATERS

Some homes will have a separate source of heat for a portion of the house added after the rest of the building, or a supplementary heater in a section that is particularly hard to heat. Homes without a central heating system will also have area heaters in the different sections of the house.

If there are self-contained space heaters, determine their number and variety. Some are perfectly safe and quite efficient. Gas-fired space heaters are much like the hot air gravity systems, only smaller and without ducts. Some rely on gravity, others have fans and are essentially simplified forced air systems.

Look first for the chimney connection for the exhaust gases. Except in cases of specially designed heaters, there must be one, as otherwise the unburned gas and exhaust fumes will poison the air of the house. Check for thermostats as well, since without them you must control the heat manually.

The classic wood stove has made a major comeback in recent years. It is a mixed blessing: wood stoves are not as clean as some other heating methods because they produce not only smoke but also soot and ash. To heat the house they have to be in a living space, and since they must be cleaned periodically, which involves transferring ash and soot from their firebox into another container, they can be messy. They can, however, be an inexpensive and efficient alternative.

The first determination you should make is whether the stove is airtight. Most new stoves are, but if the stove is older, no matter how pretty it is, it may not be airtight and could be less safe than ones that are, and is certainly much less efficient. Ask the seller if it is airtight, or close down all its vents and burn a newspaper inside (make sure the stove is connected to the flue, that the flue is open, and that the seller agrees before doing it, however). The stove is not airtight if any smoke emerges from any portion of the stove itself except the vents that control the air flow.

Some airtight stoves will burn more than twelve hours between stokings, but the older stoves that allow a freer flow of air to their fireboxes often will burn only a few hours before going out.

If a house is being heated by wood, one way to compare the cost is to ask how many cords of wood were burned in the course of the previous winter. One cord of wood roughly equates to a hundred gallons of fuel oil in the amount of heat generated.

Whether or not the stove is airtight, be sure that all materials nearby are fireproof. Local fire codes vary, but substantial clearances are necessary from all surfaces, including a fireproof surface on the floor below the stove and in front that extends outward at least eighteen inches.

Kerosene heaters can be efficient and are inexpensive, but given their portable nature, they can be dangerous: they can be kicked over and serious fires can result.

LIVING AREAS INSPECTION

When you ascend to the living spaces upstairs, check the heating units there. In the case of hot air, there will be registers or vents; in the case of hot water, traditional radiators or finned-tube baseboard radiators. The latter more efficiently distribute the heat.

Are the heat outlets located on outside walls? They should be to minimize the drafts of cold air from the exterior and to maximize the thermal currents of warm air around the room. Do there appear to be enough radiators or registers? Are they upstairs and down? Some older homes we've seen that were retrofitted for central heating systems have registers or heaters only on the first floor, which makes the upstairs areas cool indeed.

AIR-CONDITIONING SYSTEMS

Central air-conditioning is increasingly common these days, not only in the southern United States, but in northern areas as well. Like heating systems, they are expensive investments, so if you uncover matters for concern in the inspection, consult an air-conditioning expert. Inquire of the seller who installed and who has maintained the system. Again, a telephone call to them may answer most or all of your questions.

In any refrigerant system—whether it is inside your refrigerator or freezer or air conditioner—the key element is the cooling medium. The so-called refrigerant is a gas when it is at normal atmospheric pressures, but, when compressed as it is by the compressor in a cooling system, it becomes a liquid. Then, upon the release of the pressure in the system's next stage, the evaporator, the liquid will return to its gaseous state and, in the process, absorb heat.

It is at the evaporator coil that the air is cooled. A flow of air is directed by a fan over the evaporator coil which contains the pressurized liquid. The liquid draws the warmth from the air. The result is cooler air as the liquid becomes warmer and returns to its gaseous state. The cooled air is driven by a fan into the distribution system (duct work) of the house.

An air-conditioning system's constituent parts, then, are a compressor to pressure the gas into a liquid; a condenser coil that aids in that process by cooling the gas with circulated air; the evaporator coil in which the refrigerant returns to a gas; and the ducts that take the cooled air to the living areas of the house and return warmer air to the evaporator to start the process again.

Your inspection should first determine which parts of the system are located where. Often only the evaporator coil is in the house, frequently in the same plenum that distributes the warm air to the house in the warm-air heating system (you will see the curved ends of the coiled pipe peering out of the plenum's body). The compressor and condenser unit may be outdoors, located out of the direct sun but in an area that is clear of fences and shrubs so that air can flow around and through it.

Do not test the system unless the temperature outdoors is sixty degrees Fahrenheit or better. (If it is not warm enough to test the system, you should insist that the seller warrant in the sale agreement that the system is in good working order.)

Position yourself near the compressor and condenser unit. Instruct your helper to turn down the thermostat in the house that controls the air conditioner. Listen for the compressor and the fan: a constant humming noise is normal, anything else could mean trouble. Squawks or bangs suggest that an expert should be consulted. The compressor is usually the most expensive part of the system and has a probable life expectancy of ten years, depending upon the load it must carry. If the compressor and condenser are inside the home, is the noise disturbing to you in the living areas of the house?

Inspect the exterior of the unit: not only listen but look for signs of trouble like leaks or signs of corrosion. Is the unit level or has its footing settled unevenly? Is the flow of air to it obstructed by bushes or a fence?

You should also listen for starting and stopping. An air-conditioning system that is properly matched to the needs of the house should run almost constantly; if it runs in fits and starts it either needs repair or has a capacity that is too great for the house. As a result, the compressor will be constantly starting and stopping, a situation that not only causes unnecessary wear and tear on the equipment but also means that the cooled air is likely to arrive in chilly blasts rather than in a gentler, constant flow.

Look at the data plate on the compressor. It may mention the number of BTUs the system puts out. One British Thermal Unit (BTU) is the amount of heat required to raise the temperature of one pound of water one degree Fahrenheit. Another measure of cooling is the ton: one ton of air-conditioning is the cooling required to melt one ton of ice in twenty-four hours. One ton of cooling is equivalent to twelve thousand BTUs.

In a house of conventional shape and design, one ton or twelve thousand BTUs of air-conditioning is required to cool five to six hundred square feet of space. You can use this approximation to estimate whether your system is roughly adequate.

If the compressor data plate does not have the output of the system, you can use another method to calculate its cooling capacity. The amperage of the unit should be mentioned. As there are seven amps per ton of cooling, divide the amperage given by seven and you will have the tonnage. If, then, the house has two thousand plus square feet and you, therefore, require about four tons of cooling, the compressor should have an electrical load of twenty-eight amps. If the amperage is considerably more or significantly less, the capacity of the system is not ideally suited.

Check the evaporator. Usually the evaporator is located inside the plenum. It is recognizable by the ends of the coil peering out of the duct or by following the refrigerant lines from the compressor. Here, too, you should check for signs of water trouble. This part of the air-conditioning process involves condensation; it is a normal part of the operation of the air conditioner. Consequently, there will be a sump onto which the water will drain. Check for a

drain line, a plastic or copper tube that allows the condensation to drain off.

Are there any signs of rust or corrosion? Of mineral
deposits? These suggest that condensation has not been
drained off effectively, and that the rust will continue and
will eventually damage the evaporator.

If the air conditioner has run for a few minutes (allow
fifteen to twenty minutes to be sure it is fully operational),
check the registers in the living spaces of the house. Are
they all getting a flow of air? Is it significantly greater in
some areas than others? Is there little or no flow upstairs?
Are there registers in every room?

Ideally, registers for cooling systems should be located near the ceiling; for warm air, the nearer the floor
the better. Some homes have ducts built into the walls that
allow the air to be directed to a ceiling duct in the warm
weather or to a lower vent in the winter, but whatever the
arrangement in the house, you should pay close attention
to the flow of air. Are there hot and cold spots? Does the
air circulate freely? Are there rooms with no ducts at all?

INDIVIDUAL AIR CONDITIONERS

When the house is equipped with individual units installed in windows or in sleeves built into the walls of the
dwelling, be sure that your contract specifies they are to be
included in the sale; often, they are not.

If they are part of the purchase, you should inspect
and, assuming the temperature allows, also test them.
Look for signs of rust and corrosion: air conditioners not
only are subject to the elements but also the flow of moist
air and water can lead to rust. Listen for untoward noises:
a hum is normal, squawking or groaning is not. Check the
filters: if they appear not to have been cleaned for a sub-

stantial period, the machine, particularly the compressor, may have been taxed to such a degree that it is dangerously near its end.

Check the data plate for the output of the unit. The same rule of thumb applies: you need roughly twelve thousand BTUs per five hundred plus square feet of living space (assuming normal ceiling heights and average window coverage).

ASSESSMENT OF CHECKPOINT NO. 9

MISCELLANEOUS CONCERNS: If you are inspecting the house during the warmer months, there is no way to determine for sure that the heating system is up to its assignment; in the winter, the same is true of the air-conditioning. Ask the seller specifically if you have any reason for doubt, like the presence of space heaters, for example, in all the upstairs bedrooms.

IMMEDIATE IMPROVEMENT INDEX: The following problems demand your immediate attention:

I — Walls or ceilings of flammable materials in the immediate vicinity of the burner that are unprotected by gypsum board or other fireproof material;

— Insufficient ventilation in the burner area;

— The absence of a pressure-relief valve on a steam or hot water system;

— There is no emergency shutoff for the furnace or boiler;

— The absence of pressure and temperature gauges on a steam or hot water system.

II — Signs of rusted or corroded pipes in some portion of the delivery system to the house in a hot water or steam system;

— The need to replace the oil storage tank;

— Indications that a new firebox or boiler tank is necessary;

— Though not strictly necessary, converting a gravity hot air or water to a forced system will result in considerable energy savings;

— Signs that substantial maintenance will be necessary on the central air-conditioning system like clangs or bangs coming from the compressor or rust or other signs of deterioration on the evaporator coil and surrounding duct work.

III — The need to replace the boiler or furnace.

WALK-AWAY FACTORS: This is one checkpoint where you shouldn't hesitate to get an expert from the fuel company or maintenance firm that has done business with the seller to come have a look if you find evidence of things being amiss in the temperature control system(s). They can follow up your findings at this checkpoint, and perhaps save you needless worry—and warn you of serious trouble just over the horizon.

The installation of even the simplest heating systems can run into thousands of dollars, and elaborate combined heating/cooling and the attendant duct work can be ten thousand dollars or more in an average sized home. If it appears that a major overhaul of a system is in order, it may be a Walk-Away Factor, depending upon your budget for large cash outlays after the purchase of the house.

If you found no worrisome signs of trouble, your house just leaped a major hurdle. However, this is so significant an aspect of the inspection that if you have any doubts at all, get a professional evaluation.

Checkpoint No. 10

WATER, PLUMBING, AND HOT WATER HEATERS

John and Linda Jameson bought their town house in Hoboken with an inheritance from Linda's father. It was a difficult financial squeeze, but they decided the gracious old building was worth the gamble. With an apartment in the basement to let, it would provide some income to pay the sizeable monthly mortgage, and there was more than enough space for John's business and their two young children, unlike all the apartments in which they had tried to make do in years past.

But the bubble burst. Or, rather, a pipe did. Linda and John discovered to their horror shortly after closing that not merely one but all the pipes required replacement. The pipes were cast iron, their insides rusted, clogged, and weakened. The whole place had to be replumbed, and they simply didn't have the money to do it.

Becoming a master plumber takes years of training, strong hands, an organized intelligence, and a willingness to get dirty. But identifying a plumbing problem takes no expertise or training, and John or Linda could have discovered their problem in advance of their purchase. After all, a leak is a leak, to eight year olds and engineers alike.

Plumbing is all about getting the clean water in and the wastewater out—and spilling nary a drop in the process. In most homes, one pipe delivers the water to the house from the well or municipal system or other source; that pipe divides at the hot water heater, and then the cold and hot water lines feed each of the fixtures, whether it is the kitchen sink, the bathtub, the toilet, or the utility room. Once the water is used, there is a system of waste pipes that tie into one main pipe so the water leaves the house, once again, in a single pipe.

In this checkpoint, we will be looking to identify which of these pipes are which in your house, and whether there are any problems evident.

THE WATER

To begin, you must determine whether the source of water to the house is a well on the property or a municipal supply. If the source is municipal, there's probably a bill to pay (though sometimes the cost is incorporated into local taxes), but it also means many fewer potential headaches. Any troubles that develop from the point of connection with the community pipes to your own are your responsibility, but there is generally no need for an expensive pump or holding tank or pressure gauge when the supply is municipal.

Look for a "curb valve." This will shut off the supply of water to the house and is often located at the curb, as its name suggests. The name of the pipe that brings the water to the house, not dissimilar to the terminology of the electrical system, is the "house service main."

In inspecting the other hidden and mechanical portions of the house, no doubt you have seen signs of the plumbing. If you haven't noticed a storage tank or the point at which the main enters the house, follow the pipes you have seen back to their source. Whether it is well water or not, the water is most likely to arrive through a wall in the basement.

Look for a meter: usually there will be one on a municipal system. If you find no meter and instead find a pump and holding tank, odds are that you have a well. If you are unable to make the determination, ask the seller.

If the source is a well, you must have the water tested. Many banks require it, and you should, too, for the sake of your health and that of your family. Many areas of the country are increasingly reporting contaminated ground water, so you should be sure you are buying clean water. In addition, a new well can be expensive, running into thousands of dollars. If the source is municipal, you can check with the community's water department or commissioner or the board of health for its source and quality; if the source is a well and the seller is not required to have a test conducted, ask your bank's mortgage department or real estate broker to refer you to a qualified lab to test the water. If there is no source of water of an acceptable quality (standards have been established), then walk away.

Look at the pipe that appears from the wall. Check for signs of rust or corrosion and for mineral deposits on the pipe or the wall below. If the house is an older home, look for a swollen section at one of the joints, and gently tap the pipe with your hammer. A swelling that dents easily when you hammer it, called a wiped joint, indicates that the inlet pipe is made of lead.

Even in trace amounts, lead is a health hazard, so you should have the water in a system that uses lead pipes tested, regardless of whether or not it is from a well. If you suspect the pipe is lead but do not see a wiped joint, hold your screwdriver like a pen and scratch the pipe, bearing down about as hard as you would to ensure that your handwriting would carry through two or three layers of carbon paper. If the metal scratches and a shiny gray color is visible, it's lead.

Check for a shut-off valve inside the house: it is essential for working on the system. It is simply a tap that should be on the main service line just inside the house; you (or your plumber) will shut it off when replacing a faucet washer or fixing a leak.

WELLS AND PUMPS

It probably comes as no surprise to you that wells are of two basic kinds, shallow and deep. Those that are up to twenty-five feet deep are termed shallow. A well must extend to the water table, that being the point beneath the surface where ground water is found. Often deep wells reach depths of five hundred or more feet.

The pump is the key moving and mechanical part of your plumbing system. There are three different kinds, the piston pump, the jet pump, and the submersible.

The jet pump and the traditional piston pump both work by suction but they, along with submersible, must accomplish the same thing: they must provide sufficient pressure to drive the water from the source to each of the fixtures, whether it is from a ten-foot-deep cistern or a five-hundred-foot-deep well, whether it is going to a third-floor bath forty feet above or a utility sink inches away.

The submersible pump is often used in deep wells. It is located in the well at or below the water table. Rather than working by suction to draw the water to the surface (as is the case with shallow wells), it pushes the water upward via a centrifugal pumping motion.

When we go upstairs to the bathroom, we will test the

water pressure, and it is at that point that the efficiency of the pump can best be judged. However, at this checkpoint you should investigate the storage tank and the pressure switch and gauge.

The storage tank should have a pressure gauge mounted on it. As most tanks are rated for a maximum pressure of 75 psi. (pounds per square inch), it should not read more than that. (If the water source is municipal, however, the pressure may be higher.)

Most systems function on a high/low switch. You will see an electrical switch mounted on the pipe that brings the water in from the well. It is preset to turn the pump on when the pressure falls below a certain level, and to turn it off when the pressure reaches a higher plateau. Common settings are 20/40 and 30/50 psi.

Test the function of the switch and gauge by turning on a nearby faucet. After it runs a few moments, you should see the needle on the pressure gauge begin to fall. If after a few minutes it hasn't moved, the gauge is probably defective and should be replaced.

If it does fall, watch how far it falls before the pump comes on. If the pump is not located near the storage tank (as is the case with a submersible pump that can be many hundreds of feet below you), you may hear only the clicking of the pressure switch. You may also hear the rush of water entering the tank when the pump goes on, or feel the vibration of the pump in the tank.

The pump should not go on and off repeatedly. This may indicate a switching problem or, more likely, that the air that is required in the storage tank has escaped and the tank has become "waterlogged." This condition is generally not complicated or expensive to fix, but it may cause the pump to wear out considerably more quickly than under normal conditions. A Handyman may wish to take this one on; often, replacing the tank is the simplest solution.

THE HOT WATER HEATER

If cleanliness is next to godliness, then it only follows that the hot water heater is next in importance to the source of the water itself. As you inspect the pipes, you will no doubt come across a point where the cold water feed pipe divides—one pipe goes to the hot water heater, the other continues along to the sinks and other fixtures in the house.

As we found with the heating systems, there are a variety of kinds of domestic hot water heaters. They can be divided into two basic categories: the first are those that rely on the burner in the main heating system in the house, the second are totally independent systems.

Most new homes will have independent systems, but there are many older homes and even some new designs that incorporate the heating of the domestic hot water into the furnace or boiler. Look first for a cylindrical piece of equipment that is large enough to contain a holding tank of somewhere between a thirty- and eighty-gallon capacity. The most likely locations are the cellar, a utility room, the garage, or, in some cases, a closet.

If you have trouble locating the hot water heater, find the pipes that feed the kitchen or bathroom fixtures (the plumbing piping for domestic water use is usually distinguished by being smaller in diameter, an inch or less, than the heat piping for your hot water heating system). Follow one of the pipes that is hot to the touch (if none is, turn on the nearest hot water tap and let it run a few minutes). At one extreme it will feed the fixtures, at the other it will connect to the water heater.

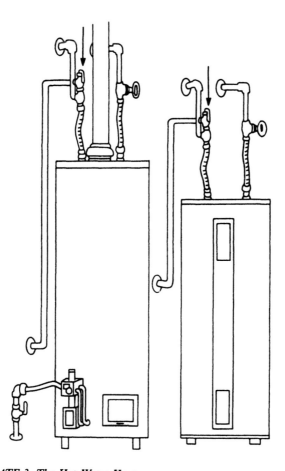

PLATE 3. The Hot Water Heater

Most hot water heaters use electricity or gas. On the right is an electric hot water heater; note the absence of a flue pipe. The gas unit on the left has an exhaust flue for fumes to escape up the chimney. Note also that there must be a temperature/pressure relief valve on the piping that leaves the heater. The arrows indicate the valve on both hot water heaters.

If the system does not have a separate water heater, then the house relies on the heat generated in the furnace or boiler or on what is called a tankless coil. If you do find a large tanklike object, make sure it has its own source of heat; it may be electric, or gas or oil fired, or it may simply be a hot water holding tank for a furnace- or boiler-fired heater.

If the hot water system is part of the furnace, you should inspect the fittings around the pipes' entrance and exit: Are there any signs of rust or leakage or corrosion or mineral deposits? Extensive wear and tear suggests some replacement or repair will be necessary. The Handyman or venturesome Apprentice may be willing to take on the simple replacement of one or two worn fittings, but if the badly deteriorated area involves part of the furnace or more than a confined area of the piping, the pros should certainly be called in.

HOT WATER OUTPUT

However the water is heated, one of your principal concerns has to be the output of the system. This capability is determined by two factors. One is how large a volume of hot water is stored in the system (assuming the system has a storage tank). The other factor is how quickly the heater can replenish the store of hot water.

Generally your household needs will be served by having water at 140° if you use automatic dish- or clothes-washing machines. Temperatures between 115° and 120° are sufficient if all of your water needs involve the human hand, as the tolerance most people have for hot water is no more than that. Heating water to greater temperatures is a waste of energy dollars.

On average, about five gallons of water will emerge

from a faucet per minute. Analyze your needs: Will you frequently have occasion to draw simultaneously from two or more hot water faucets (for purposes of this exercise, assume that the shower, the tub in the second bathroom, the dishwasher, and the clothes washer draw approximately the same amount of hot water)? How long will each run?

Multiply the five gallons per minute times the number of simultaneous demands that will be made on the system, and use that number as your maximum demand. For example, your dishwasher may demand five minutes of hot water; the clothes washer, eight minutes; Junior's shower, two minutes; and Aunt Esther's bath, five minutes, for a total maximum demand of twenty minutes. Multiplied times the five-gallons-per-minute figure, your system will have to produce a hundred gallons in that period.

Now look at the capacity of your water heater. It should be indicated on a plate on the heater. Most home water heaters have tanks that hold between thirty and eighty gallons. On the basis of storage alone, the thirty-gallon unit would seem to be rather too small for our hypothetical family, but let's go to the next step.

In the case of gas and oil heaters, you should also find on the data plate the heater's recovery rate. Typically, the recovery rate is one hundred or so gallons per hour. On an electrical heater, however, you must take the number of watts indicated on the data plate and divide by two hundred and fifty to get the recovery rate per hour. So if, say, our family has an electric heater of three thousand watts, that will deliver them twelve gallons of new hot water per hour; if their tank capacity is only thirty, then in any given hour they can expect only forty-two gallons of hot water. In that case they will have to make some changes in their lifestyles if they want to live in this house in the manner to which they have become accustomed.

INDEPENDENT WATER HEATERS

If your domestic water is heated by an independent water heater, determine first what kind it is. Oil and gas heaters will have stacks atop them that link to the chimney to vent the exhaust fumes, while electric heaters will not. (If the heater is gas or oil, check the stack carefully: Is it intact, or are there loose joints or other problems that will allow exhaust fumes to enter the air in the house?)

When at work, oil and gas heaters will have a visible flame inside the housing, and access grilles or openings to allow oxygen in to fuel the fire; electric heaters have neither flame nor vents.

All three of these varieties of water heaters are essentially sheet metal housings that contain holding tanks with heating elements. The tanks are lined (with glass, enamel, or copper to prevent corrosion), and the housings insulated to prevent heat loss.

Whatever the fuel, the water heater must have a release valve that will, in the event of a malfunction in the system, allow the water to escape safely when it gets too hot or the pressure too great. The escape valve must be activated by both pressure and temperature—one or the other is not adequate. The valve should be located on the piping that carries the heated water to the house or on the tank itself. If there is none, one must be installed. It is not a major investment, and the Handyman can easily find specific instructions on how to do it in literature on home repair.

In the case of the electric water heater, you cannot see the workings of the heater from the outside, so your test will have to be confined to checking that the water in the taps is hot and to determining mathematically the output of the system. However, in the case of a gas or oil hot water heater, you can test to be sure they work properly.

When there is little or no demand for hot water, the oil- or gas-fired hot water heater will run only intermittently, often with only the pilot burning during the intervals between firings. Consequently, you must cause the burner to come on to inspect it. Run the hot water in a sink or other fixture. After the tap draws some of the hot water from the hot water reservoir, the thermostat in the water heater should cause the heating element to fire.

Watch through the access hole in the side at the bottom of the heater (get no closer than three feet from the opening). If the burner does not fire, the pilot may be out or there may be no gas or oil. If there is a pilot flame and fuel in the tank and you get no firing after the tap has run for a few minutes, you should consult the fuel supplier or contractor who has maintained the system for the seller.

If the burner does fire, you will most likely hear a small "puff" sound, like a rapid exhalation of air from your lungs. If it is a very loud sound, or if any flame or smoke laps out of the access space or grille at the base of the unit, again you should consult a burner expert. As it burns, make sure that no fumes or exhaust gases or even substantial warm drafts are escaping from that area; they should be ventilated out through the chimney, and not into the living spaces of the house.

Note the color of the flame. If it is yellow rather than blue, it is in need of adjustment.

You should also look for drops of water or any sign of leakage in and around the water heater. More than a minor amount can mean a leak in the tank, though some condensation is to be expected, particularly if the temperature in the area where the hot water heater is located is cool or cold.

TANKLESS WATER HEATERS

Rather than having an independent unit, some homes have water heaters attached to the boilers that provide hot water or steam heat to the house. In such systems, a coil of pipe is mounted inside the boiler and water flows through it, drawing heat from the burner.

Such systems are not efficient, particularly in seasons when the boiler is not in use for heating the house. Again, an important concern is the output of the system: usually it is labeled as having the ability to heat so many gallons per hour. Occasionally such systems do have a storage tank to increase the hot water available, so be careful not to confuse this tank with a heater; it will have no fuel source (electricity, gas, or oil) and usually both the water output and input lines are connected to the boiler.

The inspection task is relatively simple here: Are there any signs of leaks, corrosion, or mineral buildup? Check for a pressure/temperature relief valve as well. It is necessary as a safety precaution.

THE PIPES

From the pump, the water will move into the main piping. The pipes that carry the water horizontally to the area beneath the fixtures (the sinks, toilets, and tub or shower) are called the "supply mains"; the pipes that carry the water up to the fixtures are the "fixture risers." Both the mains and risers are usually between 3/8" and 1" in diameter.

You may find the pipes are made of one of a number of materials, including copper, brass, galvanized iron, or plastic. The iron and brass pipes are joined by threaded fittings, while copper relies on solder joints.

The galvanized pipes are subject to a decreased water flow as a result of an accumulation of mineral deposits and rust. As a result, copper or brass piping is preferable. However, brass, too, is subject to wear and tear over time. In fact, the threads may become almost paper thin, while the length of the pipe may develop tiny, pinhole leaks. Look for signs of mineral deposits on the brass pipes. (Brass and galvanized iron pipes can be distinguished with a magnet —the magnet will be attracted to galvanized but not to the brass. Color alone is not always sufficient to distinguish between these two kinds of pipes.)

New construction today uses copper or plastic. The copper is much more expensive, lasts longer, and has no known effect on health. Plastic pipe comes in a number of styles and is quite inexpensive and easy to use. However, there is more than a little debate about how safe it is, particularly the variety known as PVC, an acronym for polyvinyl chloride. Certainly, PVC gives off toxic fumes when it burns; whether it is hazardous for everyday plumbing use is still at issue. You may find that the building code in your area either prohibits its use or limits it to cold water lines. PVC is generally white; another variety of plastic pipe, ABS, is black.

Whatever the material, your first concern is leakage. Inspect the pipes themselves, and the joists or beams or whatever they are attached to. Are there any signs of leakage? If there has been leakage previously, there will be water stains on nearby wood or cement.

As you inspect the pipes for signs of leakage, pay special attention to the fittings that link one length to the next. Copper pipes are usually held together by a solder joint called a sweat fitting; be alert for signs of leakage there. Don't be concerned at a greenish patina on the pipe. That's a by-product of the soldering process. If there are no heavy drops or accumulations of solder at the fittings, the plumbing was probably done by a professional and is secure.

Galvanized iron and brass piping both have been known to leak in the midst of their lengths as well as at their ends, so look for signs of leakage, and of flattening or bloating.

Be on the alert as well for any miscellaneous repairs. In one instance we heard about, a home buyer asked the seller what the sandwichlike devices attached to the pipes were. "They were necessary when we had an increase in water pressure when municipal water became available in the neighborhood" was the reply. "They're perfectly standard." Only later did our friend learn that the clamps were actually applied to staunch leaks in the old galvanized iron piping. Perhaps the seller knew full well that he was misrepresenting the problem, perhaps he actually believed what he said. But you should keep an eye out for a pattern of repairs that suggests a recurring problem.

If they are accessible, look with extra care at the areas immediately beneath plumbing fixtures, particularly the tub or shower. Is there any indication of water damage? When we get to Checkpoint 18 you will be looking for signs within the bathroom of the caulking breaking down, but check for indications down below as well.

If any of the pipes disappear into walls or ceilings and there is an access door nearby, be sure to open it and inspect inside. Your flashlight may be handy here.

Usually the cold and hot water lines travel side by side. This makes installation and inspection easier, but be sure they are not too close: a cold water pipe that is separated by fewer than six inches from the hot water line will draw heat from that hot water pipe. If the pipes seem to be perspiring, don't be concerned; that's not leaking, but condensation of moisture from the air. A small amount of

staining on the wood members adjacent to the pipes may
also be explained by condensation.

DRAINAGE

In later checkpoints we will check the fixtures in the
bathroom and kitchen, but while still in the vicinity of the
drainage pipes we will have a look at that system for troubles.

The hot and cold pipes we followed deliver the water
to the sinks and other fixtures; after the water is released
from the toilet or tub or sink, it obeys gravity's orders and
flows downward.

That's your first concern: as you glance at the drainpipes, make sure they are pitched so that the water will
flow down and away from the bathroom and kitchen and
toward the cesspool, sewer, or septic tank outside. A minimum pitch is a vertical drop of one half to one inch for
every horizontal foot. If the piping is not pitched properly,
solid wastes are likely to accumulate at a low point, and
will eventually cause the system to back up.

Because the wastewater requires a flow of air out of
the system as the water displaces it, the waste pipes are
larger than the hot and cold water pipes, between one and
one half and four inches in diameter. As was the case with
hot and cold water pipes, drainage pipes come in a variety
of materials. Most common in older homes is galvanized
iron; also common are lead, copper, and plastic.

Find the main drain where it leaves the building.
Check the pitch. As always, be on the alert for signs of
leakage. Look also for cleanouts: these are Y-shaped pieces
of pipe. One of the outstretched arms of the Y will end in
space, connected to nothing, but will have a threaded seal
over its mouth. That cleanout is designed so that in the

event of a blockage, it can be opened to provide access to the drainage line. If there are no cleanouts, you may find yourself with a more expensive plumber's bill in the event of a problem.

The drainpipes in the house are linked to a sewage system where the waste materials decompose. By-products of the rotting process include a variety of sewer gases. Some sewer gases have unpleasant and unhealthy odors, others, like methane, are a serious fire hazard as they are highly flammable.

In order to keep the sewer gas from returning to the house through the drainage pipes, every plumbing fixture must have what is called a trap. The trap is U-shaped. It is located beneath the drain in the sink or bathtub and is built into the toilet. Thanks again to gravity, water remains in the lower portion of the U, and functions as a water barrier between the sewer gases and the fixtures.

For the trap to work properly, there must be a vent pipe attached to the system. You probably observed this vent pipe on the roof of the house. It allows the sewer gases to escape. In addition, however, it prevents the water that runs out of the tub or toilet from siphoning off all the water in the trap.

If you found no vent line, then it is possible that there is none, and that the drainage lines have drawn the water in the traps off, so the gases are free to enter the home. More likely, however, you will find in Checkpoint 11 that the vent pipe ends in the attic. This is in violation of most building codes and it certainly is unsanitary. Get the seller to fix it before you move in.

SEWAGE

When the wastewater leaves the pipes inside your house, it goes either to a municipal sewage system or to a self-contained system on your property. Find out from the local health department or the seller which it is in the case of the house you're looking at.

If it is a municipal system, then maintenance is the town's or city's concern and not yours. However, if the system is on your property, then you must ascertain its suitability for your purposes.

Older houses may have a cesspool. A cesspool is essentially an underground cistern, most often made of brick or stone. It is usually constructed so that the liquid sewage can seep out while the solid waste matter remains. Cesspool systems are rarely installed today, and when problems develop with an old cesspool, it is usually the wisest course to install a more modern septic tank system.

More common are systems with a septic tank into which the sewage flows. The tank is usually of concrete and, like the cesspool, is buried beneath your lawn. In the case of a septic tank system, however, the liquid sewage moves from the tank to a leaching field or seepage pit. The leach field consists of a series of perforated pipes through which the waste liquids seep. The liquid will travel out of the holes in the pipe and "percolate" into the soil. When there is insufficient leaching in the available area, a seepage pit is installed to add capacity to the system.

When inspecting the yard, did you note any areas where the grass or foliage was very lush and green? Was there a sewer odor, or a wet or swampy area? If so, were these signs on the same side of the house as the outlet pipe for the drainage system? This can be a sign of trouble ahead: it may mean that the leach field or seepage pit is not up to the task of discharging its contents to the earth around and beneath it, so the wastewater is rising to the surface. Find out from the owner where he thinks the septic system is located to confirm your discovery.

One test to confirm this problem can be conducted by running the bathtub for an hour. Assuming a normal flow, more than 250 gallons of water should be pumped into the system (check, by following the drainage lines, to make sure the bathtub drains into the system since, occasionally, houses are designed so that the tub drains into a separate dry well since it contains no waste to deteriorate). If the system is overtaxed, you may discover fresh effluent from the system upon inspecting the area of yard over the tank and leach field.

GAS PIPES

You may find a gas pipe in the course of your inspection. Often there will be a meter outside that the gas company meter reader will need to get access to periodically. The gas pipe is less likely to be rusted or corroded, as it doesn't contain water, but inspect it for damage. It should be protected from the slams or bangs of the workshop or garage; if it isn't, guards should be installed.

Check the pipes for any signs of deterioration. Needless to say, the odor of gas or any other suggestion of a leak demands that you immediately find the shut-off valve and call in a qualified expert.

ASSESSMENT OF CHECKPOINT NO. 10

MISCELLANEOUS CONCERNS: Our century has seen astonishing gains in public health, in large part because of the advances made in clean drinking water and the careful disposal of wastewater. In keeping with comfort as well as health concerns, is the water potable, is there a sufficient quantity of both hot and cold water, and is the disposal system up to its assigned task?

IMMEDIATE IMPROVEMENT INDEX: If you observe any of the following problems, you should plan to take immediate action upon purchasing the house:

I — The gas or hot water heater vent pipe allows fumes or smoke to enter the air of the house rather than directing it all up the chimney;

— There is no pressure and temperature release-valve on the hot water heater;

— The flame on the hot water heater needs adjustment;

— Indications that a limited number of repairs need to be made to the pipes in the plumbing system;

— Several fixtures have no or improper traps.

II — The pump in the well must be replaced;

— A badly rusted or waterlogged storage tank must be replaced;

— The hot water heater must be replaced or overhauled;

— A number of pipes will need to be replaced;

— The vent pipe ends in the attic and must be extended through the roof, or the venting system is not working properly and some pipes must be added.

III — The well on the property is contaminated and
there is no municipal source available so you
must dig a new well;

— The sewage system is not municipal and needs to
be radically improved or replaced.

WALK-AWAY FACTORS: In a home plumbed with galvanized pipe that is several decades (or more) of age, the water flow may be reduced and the tap water often rusty. If this is the case, like John and Linda Jameson in their Hoboken town house, you may find that your entire system must be replumbed.

This will require substantial finish work on the walls in the kitchen and bathroom, as well as plumbing, so unless you have a handsome budget for repairs or the house is very underpriced, this problem is a Walk-Away Factor.

A second Walk-Away Factor is the absence of clean water. If there is no source of clean water on the property, walk away.

THE ATTIC

The last stop on the tour before going into the living areas of the house is the attic. In this checkpoint and in Checkpoint 12, we will complete the assessment of the portions of the house that, if you're lucky, will never call for your attention again.

There are three varieties of attics: the finished attic, in which the walls, floors, and ceilings are finished and, as a result, the framework of the house is obscured; the unfinished full attic where there is a floor, but the walls and roof are still open to reveal the structure; and the crawl attic which, like the crawl space foundation, requires that you get down on all fours to move about.

Determine how to get access to the attic. There may be a full stairway. Some homes have a movable ladder/ stairway arrangement that is pulled down from a hatch in an upstairs hallway. Many crawl attics have only a trap-door that requires you to climb a stepladder to reach it.

LEAKAGE

The inspection of the unfinished full attic and the crawl attic differs only in that the crawl attic is physically harder to inspect. Usually there is no floor in a crawl attic, but only exposed joists. You must be careful not to put any weight between the joists (the space is usually filled with insulation). If you do, anyone who happens to be in the room below may be rather surprised to see your foot appearing through the ceiling. In fact, nervous Rookies may prefer to conduct their inspection from the entrance to the attic, searching the attic from that vantage with a flashlight rather than trying to deal with the tricky footing.

Begin your inspection by looking for signs of moisture. Even if it is a dry time of year, look for water stains on the joistlike boards overhead (called "rafters"). Look for signs that water has leaked onto the insulation as well. Look particularly carefully in the vicinity of the chimney, if there is one, and any other breaks in the plane of the roof like exits for bathroom and kitchen vent pipes. As usual, it is transition spaces between one material or surface and another that are most likely to break down.

If you find any signs of water entering, check the rafters, joists, and other nearby wood for decay. Use your screwdriver once again as a probe. If you find some decay, determine how widespread the problem is. The leak must be staunched in any event but if the damage is only to an isolated area and none of the lumber is seriously decayed, it is likely that resurfacing the roof is sufficient.

However, if the damage is such that the strength of the structure is compromised (the wood is soft to the touch, and the rafters are bowing from the weight of the roof above), it is a major job. The surefooted Handyman may wish to take on the work involved in resurfacing the exterior roof, but serious decay in the beams may make you decide to walk away. Again, when it comes to any exterior roof work, remember that the dangers discussed at Checkpoint 4 come into play: the work will involve dangerous roof climbing.

If the attic is finished, you will have fewer clues. Key indicators are water stains, and peeling paint: water that has leaked down from above may cause blistering or peeling.

Check for minute amounts of water as well as puddles and large stains. Tiny droplets on the horizontal surfaces in the attic immediately beneath the roof may lead to the conclusion that condensation has frozen in the attic in cold weather and evaporated later. If the temperature is below freezing, run your hands along the rafters and inspect the points of the nails that protrude through the roof: Is there frost on them?

Also check the sheathing if it is plywood (the sheathing is the flat wood surface into which the shingles are nailed). If plywood was used, look to see if the inner laminated layer has separated. Check first on the north roof, as that portion will most likely delaminate first. If this has occurred, it is a sure sign that the attic is not adequately ventilated.

VENTILATION

Ventilation is crucial to preventing a buildup of condensation in the attic during cool weather and to limit the temperatures in warm. An inadequately ventilated attic can reach temperatures upward of 150° F. This can be both uncomfortable, as the heat warms the rooms below, and expensive, as your air-conditioning has an added load.

For every three hundred square feet of attic space

there should be at least one square foot of ventilation. An ideal arrangement is to have equal amounts of ventilation area in the inlet vents under the eaves in the soffit (the board facing downward beneath the eave) and at the outlets close to the peak of the roof. Look for the vents in the attic. You may not be able to see those in the eaves from inside, so have another look outside if you do not find sufficient vents.

In addition to soffit vents, you may find grilles in the gables or at the ridge of the roof. Some houses may also have turbines on their roofs. A turbine is a mechanical vent that resembles a chef's toque and draws the air out of the attic.

Installing grilles or other vents in the roof or gables is a job that a Handyman may wish to take on. However, consider once again that the work involves dangerous roof climbing which should be taken on only by the most confident and surefooted of workers.

OTHER CONCERNS

Some homes have attic fans; if yours does, make sure it works. Is it controlled by a switch that you must turn on and off by hand? A better arrangement is one that functions automatically, controlled by a thermostat. The Apprentice or Handyman may want to install one.

Check any pipes or ducts in the attic. The vent pipe from the plumbing should pass through the attic; if there is none, that is a problem because, as discussed in the last checkpoint, it means sewer gases can enter your home. If the pipe enters the attic and ends there, that, too, is a problem for the same reason. If there is a kitchen fan, its duct work may pass through the attic to the outdoors. If it terminates in the ceiling, it may be interpreted by certain small animals, like mice and rats, to be a virtual invitation. Are there animal signs?

If you noted any dips or variations in the straight lines of the roof earlier in your inspection, follow up on those observations, and look for signs of shifting in the structure. A roof constructed of wood members that are of insufficient size and strength for the load (a not uncommon occurrence in the Snowbelt), you may be able actually to see the bow in the roof. A serious bow in the roof, particularly in a house that is only a few years old, is a Walk-Away Factor.

If the chimney passes through the attic, check it for loose bricks, crumbling mortar, and other signs of deterioration. Sticky, dark brown stains are probably creosote and suggest that the flue lining is not intact, a fire hazard. Are there signs of charred wood around the chimney? This may indicate a chimney fire in the past. Try and determine if all the damage was repaired. Again, it is around chimneys where leakage is often found, so look carefully for decay and water stains.

Check chimneys and other stacks (you may find a metal, insulated prefabricated stack that comes from the furnace) for any signs that smoke has escaped. Make sure, too, that no chimney of any kind is in direct contact with the wood of the building: no wood should be closer than two inches to a chimney. Finally, make sure the passageway through which the chimneys arrive in the attic are closed at floor level—it should be of a fireproof material like sheet metal, but if no material is there, a fire-stop should be installed to prevent a fire below from rushing to the attic and spreading.

Does the attic you have just searched cover the entire house? Particularly in homes that have had additions to the original structure, there are often separate attics. Don't miss the attic of an entire section of the house because you don't see it from the one you inspect first.

ASSESSMENT OF CHECKPOINT NO. 11

MISCELLANEOUS CONCERNS: Your major concerns here are leakage and proper ventilation: if you found none of the former and ample of the later, the home probably passed the test at this checkpoint.

Keep in mind, however, that you will be able to store only materials that you can fit through the opening so, as usual, make sure you think carefully about what you expect of the attic—and make sure this one lives up to your needs.

IMMEDIATE IMPROVEMENT INDEX: You should plan on trying to solve the following problems if you find them:

I — The absence of fire-stops around the entrance of the chimney or furnace vent pipe at the attic floor.

II — Inadequate ventilation in the attic that means you must install vents or louvers;

— Indications (stains, etc.) of some leakage in the attic that suggest that some roof work must be done (see Checkpoint 4);

— Signs of chimney trouble like missing mortar or creosote stains.

III — Signs of very serious leakage means that a good deal of roof work must be done.

WALK-AWAY FACTORS: As we mentioned, when the roof has an evident bow in it and the house is relatively new, walk away. This symptom indicates lumber of insufficient size and strength was used and there is no reason to think that the same is not true in other, less visible areas of the house. In an old house, if the bow is barely perceptible, it is unlikely to be a matter for concern, unless the bow is caused by serious decay in the lumber. In that case, you would do best to walk away from what will be substantial repair bills.

Checkpoint No. 12

INSULATION

If the house you are inspecting was built more than ten years ago, the odds are that its insulation is inadequate. Prior to the rapid increase in energy costs that began with the oil crisis in the early seventies, a substantial insulation barrier was an uneconomical investment: the cost of heating a home, year-in, year-out was less than the onetime installation cost of insulation.

Things have changed. These days people pay attention to positioning houses with respect to the sun. New hot water heaters and other home appliances are required by law to carry an energy efficiency rating. And today the strategy for insulating residential structures is entirely different than it was as recently as the Nixon years.

In fact, the economics of the matter have been reversed: the odds are very good that today the investment involved in making your home more energy-efficient will be cost-efficient, often in a surprisingly short period.

YOUR INSULATION NEEDS

If you live in Los Angeles, your needs are quite different from those of your cousin in Portland, Maine. So the first step in determining whether your home is adequately insulated is to consult the map that indicates the insulation needs of homes in different regions of the country.

Each section of the country has been assigned a set of "R-values." An "R-value" is a measure of insulating capability. If you live in St. Paul, Minnesota, for example, the ceiling of your home should have insulation with an R-value of 38; the walls with insulation of a R-19; the floor

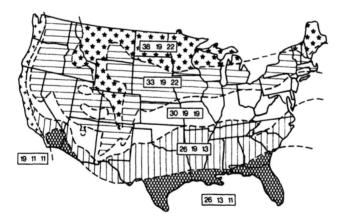

PLATE 4. Recommended Insulation Values

Different thicknesses of insulation are required in different climates. This map indicates the respective R-factors for insulation in the ceiling, exterior walls, and floors for the continental United States.

with R-22. Consult the map to determine your insulation needs before embarking upon your inspection.

When you look at the chart that identifies the R-value of the various thicknesses of the different kinds of insulation, be sure when you measure the thickness you are not measuring width; you should be determining the dimension of the insulation between the exterior and interior surfaces, whether it is the wall, ceiling, or floor.

R-RATINGS OF VARIOUS INSULATIONS

Insulation Type	R Number					
	11	13	19	22	30	38
			(in inches)			
Batts and Blankets						
Fiberglass	3.5	4	6	7	9.5	12
Rock Wool	3	4	5.5	6	8.5	11
Loose Fill						
Fiberglass	5	5.5	8.5	10	13.5	17
Rock Wool	4	4.5	6.5	9	10.5	13
Cellulose	3	3.5	5.5	6	8.5	11
Vermiculite	5	6	9	10	14	18
Rigid Board						
Polystyrene	3	3.5	5	5.5	7.5	9.5
Urethane	2	2	3.5	3.5	5	6
Fiberglass	3	3.5	5	5.5	7.5	9.5

The purpose of insulation is simple: it is to insulate you from the cold outside as well as to seal in the heat that your heating system generates. An appropriate insulation barrier will conserve energy since any lost heat—or cool, in the case of air-conditioning—translates into energy that must be used to make up for the loss.

Begin your search for insulation in the attic. Try to get access to the insulation on its floor. If it is a crawl attic, this is no problem because the insulation will be visible between the joists. If there is a floor, perhaps there is a board that can be easily pried up to see what is below. If there is no insulation in the attic and you can get access to the spaces between the joists, the Apprentice or Handyman can take on the job of installing some.

Was there insulation visible in the basement ceiling? How about in the basement stairwell, or in transition rooms between sections of the house?

As you go through the interior section of the inspection process, keep an eye out for unfinished areas in closets or elsewhere to determine what the insulation barrier is in the outside walls. Sometimes you can see into the walls by removing the plate that covers electrical switches or plugs (after cutting the power to that circuit by shutting off the appropriate breaker or fuse).

Unfortunately, it is entirely possible that you will not be able actually to measure the insulation in the walls. If that is the case, your best bet is to feel the wall on a cold day when the furnace is functioning: if the wall is cooler than the air in the room, added insulation is almost certainly needed.

You can also inquire of the seller his best knowledge of the insulation. He may not know, however. The more specific you can be in your questioning, particularly if he has installed any insulation while he lived there, the more likely you are to get accurate, valid information. Ask to see receipts from the job if he has them, and check the thickness and/or R-rating of the insulation that was installed.

As you look at the insulation, pay attention to its

condition as well as its thickness. If it has worked loose and is not tightly fitted into the bays between the structural members of the house; if it has been compressed by heavy objects being stored on top of it; or if it has evidently deteriorated in any way; then it has lost some of its effectiveness and may need to be replaced. Are there any substantial uninsulated areas, or missing pieces?

Adding insulation to finished walls and ceilings requires special equipment for blowing in insulation (see pp. 147–48). Consequently, this is to be left to the contractors who have the specialized machinery needed for the task.

Be careful not to inhale the tiny dust and glass particles that you may find in the vicinity of certain kinds of insulation. It is recommended that you purchase a simple face mask at your local hardware store if you have any lung problems or if you spend more than a few minutes in a confined space with loose fill or fiberglass insulation.

VARIETIES OF INSULATION

BATTS AND BLANKETS: The most common type of insulation found in homes constructed in recent decades is batts and blankets. After installation, the batts and blankets are virtually indistinguishable: they have the consistency of cotton fibers and the shape of a giant artificial sponge. Depending upon the material of which the insulation is made and its intended use, batt and blanket insulation may or may not have paper or foil on its surface, called a facing.

Today, fiberglass is the most common batt or blanket insulation, though you may find rock wool, cellulose (wood) fibers, or cotton that has been treated to resist fire and decay. This type of insulation is commonly manufactured in a variety of lengths and widths to fit into the standardized spacing between wall studs, floor joists, and roof rafters (widths of sixteen and twenty-four inches are most common). However, the crucial consideration for all varieties of insulation is its thickness.

LOOSE FILL: Once again, fiberglass is the most common material used as loose fill. You are most likely to find this type of insulation in your attic between the wood joists on the floor. Unlike blankets or batts, loose fill does not retain its shape when unconfined. Consequently, it can be used only where gravity can be relied upon to hold it within a space. It is generally poured into place and is often used in older homes that originally had no insulation since it can be blown through holes in the exterior walls of the home, thereby avoiding elaborate and expensive removal of interior walls.

Blown-in treated paper and formiculite are other varieties of loose fill. Paper insulation is highly efficient, more so than the rock fiber also used in these applications. In either case, however, the fill may have settled and have lost efficiency. The best way to determine whether this has happened is to get access to the heating bills for several past winters and compare them. Another way is to find out how long the fill has been in the walls: decades-old fill is much more likely to have settled than what was installed only last fall.

RIGID INSULATION: Rigid insulation comes in stiff panels, often made of urethane, polystyrene, and even fiberglass and wood fiberboard. This insulation is most often found insulating masonry walls. It is not, however, fire-resistant, so you should be sure that there is at least a half inch thickness of gypsum wallboard between it and the interior of your home to act as a fire barrier.

UREA-FORMALDEHYDE FOAM: This controversial insulation, urea-formaldehyde foam, is frequently used to retrofit older, uninsulated homes. Like loose fill, it is pumped into the walls of the house to avoid the need of costly interior wall work. However, this variety must be installed by someone who is trained and experienced in its use. And it must not be used in ceilings and attics.

The reported problems are that it can lose its effectiveness in high temperatures and humidity. In addition, when improperly installed it can release poisonous formaldehyde vapors. Headaches and other discomforts can result. Many homes have had and others still are having this urea-formaldehyde foam installed despite recent debate about its safety. It is, however, an efficient insulator and an economical alternative in some circumstances.

THE VAPOR BARRIER

An often overlooked but important element in the insulation of a home is the vapor barrier. It consists of a watertight material, most often plastic, though aluminum foil and asphalt-impregnated paper are also commonly used (the foil facing found on some insulation acts as a vapor barrier).

The vapor barrier must be on the inside of the insulation in the ceilings, floors, and walls. Its purpose is to prevent a moisture problem inside the walls. If the moisture normally found inside the home is allowed to commute to the cooler surfaces outside the insulation, it will condense. And condensation can lead to the kinds of water and decay problems discussed in earlier checkpoints. There should be only one barrier, on the inside of the wall; if there are two, chances are there will be some condensation problems.

Look for the vapor barrier as you look for the insulation; its absence can mean a significant increase in maintenance problems with the home because of a moisture buildup in the walls and attic. Unfortunately, it is prohibitively expensive to add a barrier to most finished homes.

PIPES AND DUCTS

In unheated portions of the house, all pipes and ducts should be insulated. A thickness of one to two inches is commonly found; more is often better in sections of the country where the winters are long and cold. If there is no insulation around the pipes or ducts, it can be added at relatively small expense, but it can make a significant contribution to reducing the heating costs of the home. Apprentices and even Rookies will find this job within their reach.

Don't forget to check the garage where it is part of the house, particularly in a raised ranch design. Ducts here typically pass through the garage on the way to the upstairs bedrooms. They, too, should be insulated.

If there is central air-conditioning in the home, there should be a vapor barrier around its duct work to prevent condensation. In this case, the insulation is more a matter of proper maintenance than of a cost saving, as the condensation can lead to rust and deterioration of the ducts.

ASSESSMENT OF CHECKPOINT NO. 12

MISCELLANEOUS CONCERNS: Your judgment of the safety and soundness of the house should be relatively unaffected by your findings at this checkpoint. Rather, the presence (or absence) of sufficient insulation, a vapor barrier, and other protections are a matter of dollars and cents. But given the continuing increases in the cost of energy, this cost may be even more significant in the coming years than it is today.

IMMEDIATE IMPROVEMENT INDEX: Addressing the following matters, while not essential for safety or comfort, will improve the energy efficiency of the home:

I — The absence of insulation around the duct work of a central air-conditioning system.

II — The absence of insulation in the unfinished or crawl attic of the house.

III — The absence of insulation in the walls of the home.

WALK-AWAY FACTORS: Again, the absence of insulation of the home is a matter of economics. If your budgeting tells you that you must stretch to your financial limits to make the monthly mortgage payment and if the house is uninsulated and you live in a part of the country where you need to use the heating or air-conditioning systems for a significant portion of the year, you may want to walk away.

Part III

THE
LIVING
AREAS

Checkpoint No. 13

FIREPLACES
AND CHIMNEYS

For those homes that have chimneys and fireplaces, this checkpoint provides a transition to the living areas in the home. A typical masonry chimney, given its considerable weight, is firmly grounded yet reaches for the sky. Along the way, it can provide warmth and atmosphere to the home.

We'll begin this checkpoint by recapping: when you were examining the roof, you also inspected the chimney. Did you note any signs of deterioration of the bricks or mortar? Did the chimney clear the roofline as specified in Checkpoint 4? Were there any other problems uncovered there?

When you were examining the foundation (Checkpoint 6) and the heating system (Checkpoint 9), you inspected the footing or base of the chimney and fireplace. Were there any evident problems? In the attic, was the masonry intact? Did you notice any signs of uneven settlement at any point? Was there any creosote on the side of the chimney that leaked through the flue lining?

THE CHIMNEY

A fireplace may be romantic but it is not an efficient way to heat your home. A fireplace draws air from the room into the firebox where the fuel is located to provide the flame with the oxygen it needs to burn. The result is the generation of heat, but much of it is drawn up the chimney. To make matters worse, if there is another source of heat in the home, then some of that warm air is drawn into the fireplace and it too is lost. The efficiency of a typical fireplace is between 5 and 25 percent.

Begin your inspection of the fireplaces in the home by looking at the exterior of the fireplace. If you noted on your Checksheet earlier that the chimney visible on the roof angled strangely, look particularly carefully here for other signs of trouble. Is the masonry intact? Is there any mortar missing? If such signs of deterioration are evident, try and determine whether the problems are simply with the surface bricks or if the trouble extends to structure of the fireplace or chimney. Superficial work is a matter of repointing and, while messy, it rates only a *II* on the Index. Serious structural trouble with the chimney can be a Walk-Away Factor.

Are there any smoke stains on the front of the fireplace, immediately above the opening of the firebox? If so, this suggests that the fireplace is smoky. There may be a number of explanations for this, including downdrafts or poor chimney design. However, the problem is probably more an issue of cleanliness than of safety: smoke that enters the home will leave soot and ashes on shelves and windowsills and other surfaces. If the fireplace is extremely smoky, however—and the only way to know is to test it— it can be a health hazard as inhaling quantities of wood smoke is harmful to the lungs.

Are there any signs in the firebox of use like soot or ash? If not, perhaps it is not a functional fireplace and is only there for appearances. Ask the seller.

Look up the chimney: Is there a damper? A damper is usually metal, and it is a method of closing the flue to prevent the warm air in the house from going up the chimney when the fireplace is not in use and to prevent uninvited squirrels and chipmunks from dropping in. A damper is not absolutely essential (and is not to be found in many older homes) but is an economical and useful feature that should be installed if there is none. Test it: Does it work easily or is it rusted in one position?

Perhaps the single most important safety consideration in any chimney is the flue lining. A chimney constructed today must have a lining of an inflammable substance, usually tile. Look up the chimney; use your flashlight to discern the lining if you need. Is the chimney lined with tile or can you discern brick and mortar? If there is no flue lining, you should hire an experienced chimney sweep to clean and then inspect the chimney carefully, as it may not be safe.

THE FIREBOX

Inspect the firebox. Again, are there any signs of broken or chipped bricks or crumbling mortar? The highest temperatures are reached in the firebox, so the condition of the masonry is crucial here. Are there signs that the pointing or the bricks themselves in the firebox are worn and might allow smoke, heat, or even fire to escape the firebox and enter the framing of the dwelling?

Look up the flue: Are there any obstructions apparent? Sometimes because of the design of the chimney you may not be able to see light above. Check with the seller first, but you may want to burn a piece of newspaper to check the flue and the draft.

If a wood stove is attached to the fireplace, inspect it according to the procedure outlined in Checkpoint 9. The same inspection process applies to a fireplace–insert wood stove that is actually built into the fireplace opening.

ASSESSMENT OF CHECKPOINT NO. 13

MISCELLANEOUS CONCERNS: Safety is all important here: Did you uncover any indications that the fireplace is unsafe? If so, do not hesitate to get a professional examination of the flue and firebox. Many local fire departments will perform this service for free.

As for taking on the various tasks involved in chimney maintenance, you will probably discover that the tools required for cleaning cost more than hiring an expert to come and do it for you. Plus, he takes the roof-walking risks—and saves you trouble of doing one of the world's dirtiest jobs.

As for lining or relining work, that too takes special equipment and skills. In addition, your city or state fire or building codes may require that the work be done by a certified professional. For all but the experienced Handyman or mason, chimney work is best left to the experts.

Aesthetic concerns are also important, given the sheer size and the visual impact a fireplace can have. Do you like the design and material of the fireplace? A rough-hewn stone fireplace can be a perfect match for plain country decor, but can look very out of place amid a roomful of formal furniture.

IMMEDIATE IMPROVEMENT INDEX: The following problems require your immediate concern:

I — A chimney with an evident accumulation of creosote must be cleaned.

II — Two or more chimneys that need to be cleaned;

— A chimney that requires lining or a firebox that needs repointing;

— While not essential for safety reasons, it would be wise to install a damper in a fireplace without one.

III — More than one chimney with unlined flues;

— A chimney whose foundation has settled and that needs substantial reconstruction.

WALK-AWAY FACTOR: If the principal source of heat for the home utilizes a chimney (or chimneys) that are not safe, get a contractor's estimate for correction of the problem or walk away.

If the house is old and there are several chimneys and all of them are in poor condition and will require substantial reconstruction, you may also elect to walk on to the next house on your real estate agent's list. Chimney work is expensive, especially when the chimneys are inside the framing of the house and the work requires opening up walls and floors and ceilings for access.

Checkpoint No. 14

FLOORS

The floors should be inspected along with the doors, windows, walls, and ceilings as you walk through the living spaces of the house. The floors should be flat and level: Is there a pronounced pitch from one side of a room to the other, or is there a sag at the center? Are there any stains? Most often, stains suggest the past presence of water on the floors.

Do the floors squeak? Often an occasional complaint is to be heard from the floors in a home, and it suggests a loose floorboard or two. This can be corrected by the Apprentice or Handyman armed with a hammer and the proper nails. But if the squeaking is found everywhere, it may be symptomatic of a larger problem.

If the floor seems sound, you may gently jump up and down on them. Do any of the floors give noticeably when you land? They shouldn't, so if they do it may mean the floor joists beneath are of insufficient size and strength for the load. There is virtually no likelihood that the floors will give way, but a sag may well develop in a newer home where the floors have give in them. Short of major reconstruction, there is little to be done.

If you observe any slant or curvature or excessive give or squeak, you should go to the floor below and examine the structure beneath the floor. (If you have any doubt as to how level the floor is, rest a marble or golf ball in various spots around the room. If it rolls on its own, the floor is not level.) Does the ceiling reveal any signs of the trouble above? If not, then it is likely that the variation in pitch is attributable to normal settlement of the structure or to shrinkage of the lumber used in the building, also a usual circumstance.

If the signs of trouble on the floor above lead you back to the basement (and if the structure is not hidden by a finished ceiling), you will find horizontal beams and joists. The beams are the larger of the two. When viewed from the end, they are either square pieces of solid timber, often 6″ × 6″ or larger, or are made up of two or more pieces of dimension lumber fastened together (2″ × 6″ or 2″ × 8″ or 2″ × 10″ or more).

The joists rest on the beams, extending at right angles from one beam to another. Joists are commonly 2″ × 8″ or 2″ × 10″ (the longer dimension is always vertical for greater strength), and spaced at 12″ or 16″ or 24″ intervals. The span of a 2″ × 8″ joist should be no more than 12′ without a supporting beam breaking up its length; 2″ × 10″ should not reach more than an uninterrupted 14′. Again, if you find lumber of insufficient dimension there is little to be done at this late date.

On top of the joists there should be a subfloor. In older homes the subfloor consists of plain boards nailed to the joists diagonally across the room; in recent construction, the subfloor is more likely to be plywood or some other form of sheet board.

As you look up at the joists, you should look for signs of shifting: Are there places where the weight on the floor above or the changes in the building's shape have led to one or more of the joists shifting out of alignment? Instead of being perpendicular, perhaps one or more joists sits oddly, tilting to one side or the other. Once again, there is virtually no chance of the floor giving way, but unsightly and inconvenient variations in the level surface of the floor may well result.

Is there cross bridging between the joists? Cross bridging, a standard construction technique used to avoid such shifting, is the nailing of pairs of smaller dimension boards in an X pattern between the joists. If there is no cross bridging you may find block bridging, in which the same dimension lumber as was used for the joists has been nailed, in a blocklike way, between the joists. The absence of any sort of bridging suggests that the builder of the house cut corners.

WOOD FLOORS

Wood floors can be beautiful and durable. They have a warmth, both literal and visual, that can enhance the comfort of a room.

You will find that wood floors come in three basic types: strips, planks, and blocks. Strips are roughly two inches wide, the planks more than three and a half inches in width. The blocks, sometimes made of short, solid lengths of strip flooring and sometimes of hardwood plies laminated together, are rather like tiles and are used for parquet pattern floors.

In general, the harder the wood the better the floor. Oak is the most commonly used hardwood for floors, but maple and birch and other hardwoods are also very resistant to surface damage. Some softwoods like western Douglas pine are often used for floors, but they are softer

and their surfaces scratch more easily. Generally softwoods can be distinguished from hard by the presence of
knots and a yellowish tinge.

In your inspection of wood floors, look for any signs
of scratches or mars. Superficial markings in the wax can
be easily covered and can usually be distinguished from
more serious damage by rubbing a moistened finger over
the spot. Markings that cut more deeply into the floor may
require refinishing or even resanding. Look with special
care at areas where chairs are likely to be moved often, as
is the case around kitchen and dining room tables.

Inspect wood floors for signs of cupping or buckling.
Cupping—where a single board curves upward—occurs
when the floorboard is wet for a prolonged period. In the
event a large area of the floor is wet, buckling can also
occur, when two boards, swollen with dampness, no longer
fit into their allotted space and rise up to form a ridge.

Wood shrinks over time, so you should expect older,
wide-board floors to cup or bow and for cracks to open at
their edges. Examine flat wide-board floors in houses that
are more than a century old to be certain that the boards
have not been sanded paper thin at the edges.

Many people find that wood floors are not satisfactory
in kitchens or bathrooms, as the high humidity and frequent water spillage that are inevitable in those rooms can
lead to an erosion of the finish, unsightly watermarks, and
even decay when the problems are not addressed. Consequently, do not be surprised if you find signs of such wear
and tear on wooden floors in bathrooms and kitchens, and
you may want to consider budgeting some money for covering them with a more water-repellent surface like one of
those we are going to discuss.

TILE AND FLEXIBLE FLOORING

TILE FLOORS: As with wood, there are an almost endless variety of tile surfaces. Some are expensive and some not, but tiles are generally durable and easy to clean.

Most often tile floors are found in bathrooms or kitchens. The tiles are usually made of a ceramic material like clay that has been baked at very high temperatures in a kiln. Most tiles are water- and stain-resistant; they may have a surface glaze or not. Ceramic mosaic tile and quarry tile are not glazed and are most often used on floors. Beware of brand-new glazed tiles with a glossy finish: they should be used only on lightly trod upon floors as outdoor grit and other abrasive materials are likely to scratch their surface. Glazed tiles for floor applications generally have a dull or matte finish.

Despite their durability, some people find that certain kinds of stone or tile floors, specifically those made of hardened ceramics and other rock-hard materials, are unsatisfactory. One objection is that they are unforgiving when breakables are dropped onto them: a dish that might survive a fall onto a wood surface will very likely shatter upon contact with tile.

In the case of hardened tile floors, you should inspect extra carefully for hairline cracks and other signs of breakage. When the subfloor beneath these tiles is other than totally rigid, they often break rather than flex with the movement of the floor. Check the adhesive used: Is there cracked or missing adhesive in the joints between the tiles? Ask the seller if he has additional tiles from the same lot. These should be passed along with the house in case replacements are needed. Even the Rookie can easily learn the process of chipping out the old tile and grout, and replacing them with new.

FLEXIBLE FLOORING: Flexible flooring (also referred to as resilient flooring) is a category of thin floor surfaces whose best known variety is linoleum. Manufactured of vinyl and of various fibers, flexible flooring is an inexpensive alternative to tile floors. At its best, this category of floors is durable, carefree, and waterproof.

Flexible flooring comes in sheets and in tiles. It comes in rolls with foam cores and in more nearly rigid, vinyl-asbestos tiles. Rubber and cork are occasionally used as flexible floor surfaces, as are other materials.

When inspecting flexible flooring, look for broken tiles and cracks. Look for gaps between the floor surface and the edges of the walls or islands. Look for stains and other signs of wear and tear. Look for variations in the surface: Does the floor lie flat, or are there rolling hills and dales? (This effect is most likely in sheet vinyl floors applied by an amateur.) Are the tiles laid in a consistent pattern? Do the seams of the sheets align?

WALL-TO-WALL CARPETING

Check the nap or pile of the carpet: Is it of consistent depth or are there sections where it has worn thin? If you can see the pattern of the roughly woven material into which the nap has been sewn, the carpet is probably well worn and may need replacement shortly.

Are there stains? Look carefully at areas of maximum wear, such as entrances and exits, the most direct paths through one room to the next, and in eating areas.

In rooms with wall-to-wall carpeting, do not assume that there is a wood or other finished floor surface beneath. It is common practice today to install carpeting directly on subflooring. Even if the adjacent room has a handsome wood floor, that is no indication that the carpet in the one next door hides one, too.

ASSESSMENT OF CHECKPOINT NO. 14

MISCELLANEOUS CONCERNS: Do the floors seem sturdy? If they seem structurally sound, then the issue becomes one of personal taste. Do you like the floor materials? Will they suffice for your family's needs?

IMMEDIATE IMPROVEMENT INDEX: These problems demand your attention:

I — Flexible flooring that needs to be replaced in one room.

II — Wood floors with boards that have cupped or buckled and may trip you or visitors, or boards whose edges are worn unevenly so bare feet may get slivers from them and that must be sanded and refinished;

— Tile floors in which numerous tiles are cracked and broken, especially in bathrooms and kitchens where water is often on the floor and may seep through to wood structural members that could decay.

III — A wood or tile floor that must be taken up and completely replaced because it is deteriorated beyond repair.

WALK-AWAY FACTORS: If you find signs that much of the floor in the house is uneven, especially if it sags in the middle or if the joists you can see from below have evidently shifted, return to the checkpoints for the attic, foundation, and exterior wall surfaces. You should find signs there, as well, of uneven settlement or shifting. If so, you would do well to walk away from a house that is only a few years old. On the other hand, a very old house is likely to have a good deal of variation in its levels and squares, so the sags and shifts are to be expected.

INTERIOR WALLS
AND CEILINGS

Most walls and ceilings aspire to the condition of flatness. Interior walls and ceilings should be sturdy and durable, but practicality and appearance are more important criteria for judging inside surfaces. Smoothness, too, is usually a virtue in walls, as blisters, bumps, and bulges suggest trouble.

Another consideration in assessing walls and ceilings is that some materials require more maintenance than others, particularly in situations where more moisture is present more of the time, as is the case in kitchens and bathrooms.

When inspecting the walls, make sure you look at all of them. While three of the four walls in a given room may be in perfect condition, the fourth could be in need of considerable repair. And imagine them empty of pictures and posters. If possible, look behind the couch and the dressers, checking for surface variations that are unsightly or will require repairs. If you see signs of recent repair work, like plaster of a different texture or patches of joint compound, be wary. That suggests a problem has been covered up, perhaps after it was cured, perhaps not. Ask the seller.

Note the presence or absence of electrical outlets (also called plugs or receptacles). Building codes today call for receptacles at no more than six-foot intervals; you may not require that many (and older homes are unlikely to have them at such frequent intervals), but make sure there are ample plugs. One house we inspected in Chevy Chase, Maryland, had none in the master bedroom, so don't take them for granted. Make sure all the plugs have protective plates on them as well.

Eye the length of the walls as you did the exterior siding, looking for signs of trouble. If you saw any signs of leakage in the attic above or in the basement immediately below, follow up those observations with an inspection of the walls and ceilings in the same general vicinity: Are there any signs of water damage, like water stains or peeling or blistering paint?

Water that has leaked into an attic may travel some distance along a rafter or ceiling before emerging in the room below, so do not be surprised if the leak you found upstairs is not apparent immediately below but there is a water problem some distance away, even in another room. Water damage can be sustained within the walls while little or no evidence is to be seen in the living areas, so follow up any clue carefully. The key is to find the problem. Once it is found, it can be dealt with, and the chances are high that the leak hasn't existed long enough to cause decay.

Do you like the finish? Repainting is a task a Rookie can do, but it takes time and costs money. If the walls are covered with wallpaper, there is at least a fifty-fifty chance that you will have to remove what's there to get a new layer to lay flat; if you want to paint them, you may have to do considerable patching of the surface beneath to get a smooth, uniform appearance.

WALL AND CEILING SURFACES

GYPSUM BOARD: The most common wall and ceiling finish found in residential construction today is called by various names, most often Sheetrock or drywall. Gypsum board is a layer of pressed plaster sandwiched between sheets of impregnated paper. It is stable, resistant to fire, and is an effective sound barrier.

In fact, gypsum board is a contemporary version of the older craft of plastering. Only instead of hiring a plasterer to trowel a layer of thick plaster onto a base of thin, narrow boards (lath) or wire mesh, sheets of gypsum board (often four by eight feet) are attached by nails or screws.

The space between each sheet is then filled with a special tape and plasterlike joint compound. Unlike plaster, gypsum board is not well suited to decorative and curved surfaces and its texture is, to some, less attractive. However, gypsum board is less likely to crack than is plaster, and it is generally less labor-intensive and less expensive to install. The strong-backed Apprentice may well want to take on a drywall project (the Handyman probably already has). The basic tools are inexpensive, and the skills, while requiring some practice, can be learned from a number of generally available how-to publications. When done well, gypsum board is a very handsome and durable surface.

Check for nail or screw heads popping through, a sign that the sheets of gypsum board may have shifted. Look also for the tape between the sheets; if you can see it, then the work was not first-class.

PANELING: Another surface often used for walls that comes in sheet form is plywood or hardboard paneling. It comes in various thicknesses, ranging from 1/8" to 3/4", faced with a variety of veneers, including softwood or hardwood and wood-grained vinyl. Given its relatively low cost and the ease with which it can be installed (roughly the same level of skills is required as for drywall work, only paneling is less time-consuming to hang), many people find it a sensible alternative to replastering an old wall, or to starting from scratch in a previously unfinished area. Again, this is within the realm of the typical Apprentice and certainly of the Handyman.

Check the paneling for strength: the thinner varieties should be mounted on a suitable framework of studding or other subwall, but often they are not. Press gently along the length of the wall at six-inch intervals. If there is a noticeable give, the paneling was probably too thin for the application and may buckle or break if a piece of furniture or a human shoulder happens to be thrust into it.

Check for sizing problems. Paneling not adequately acclimated to the atmospheric conditions in a room may swell or shrink. Is there buckling? Are there noticeable spaces between sheets?

As a matter of appearance, is it obvious to you how the paneling was attached or were the nails or other fasteners properly obscured?

WOOD BOARD PANELING: Many older homes have wood wainscoting or other wood board paneling, sometimes on the ceiling as well as the walls. The wood may be of commonplace material like pine or another softwood, or more exotic tropical woods. Thicknesses vary as well, usually between 3/8" and 3/4". Aged barn board is becoming increasingly common.

As with plywood paneling, look for sizing problems. Look for the quality of the finish work: Are the nails or glues evident?

MASONRY: Occasionally masonry is used on an interior wall surface. Sometimes the brick or stonework is the interior side of a structural wall, other times it is added for appearances only. In either case, your inspection here, as in Checkpoint 2, should concern its condition. Is the mortar intact, or is it cracking and crumbling? Do the stones or bricks show any signs of efflorescence or of any moisture accumulating?

MOLDINGS AND TRIM

Trim and moldings often add visual appeal to wall and ceiling surfaces. Most likely, however, they are there as transition materials from one material or surface to another. They provide a visual link between, for example, the ceiling and the wall, particularly when different materials are used, acting to conceal the joint as well as to decorate.

The most common moldings are cornice, baseboard, and window and door trim. The cornice moldings are found at the intersections of the ceiling and walls, the baseboard at the floor/wall joint. Also found in some homes are chair rails and picture moldings. Chair rails are intended to protect the wall surface from the backs of chairs, particularly in plaster-walled dining rooms. Picture moldings are found an inch or so below the cornice molding and offer support for picture hooks. They date from the days when pictures were generally hung with cords and hooks.

Today most moldings are made of wood but plaster cast moldings are often found in nineteenth-century homes. Check to see that the moldings are intact, that no pieces are missing. Do they fit tightly? Are the corner joints neatly fitted? Should there be molding where there presently is none? Putting in interior trim is time-consuming and exacting work, and a corner that contractors sometimes try to cut.

Another consideration is that in older homes, interior trim often consisted of a number of separate, painstakingly cut and fitted pieces or of a single, elaborately planed piece. Today the same problems are resolved with simpler pieces. Today's plain, single-piece baseboard or cornice molding will probably cover the joint between surfaces efficiently, but it usually has a good deal less visual appeal than the older, more elaborate moldings. Molding work is best left to the Handyman in the case of older houses where the molding combinations are complex. In more recent homes, molding work is within the reach of the Apprentice willing to invest in a miter box and some extra molding to experiment with.

The trim around the windows is called casing. Inspect by eye to be sure it, too, fits tightly and evenly around the window frames, and look for signs of leakage.

ASSESSMENT OF CHECKPOINT NO. 15

MISCELLANEOUS CONCERNS: Did you find any signs of trouble, particularly of water? If not, then your determinations are more subjective, having to do with whether you like the color and texture and overall appearance of the surface material.

Another issue to consider is soundproofing. In newer construction, walls are less likely to provide the sound barrier the walls in an older home will. Close the doors in one room and get someone to make noises of various levels in nearby and distant rooms. How well can you hear them?

IMMEDIATE IMPROVEMENT INDEX: These interior wall problems figure in the Index:

I — One or two average-sized rooms require repainting and you will be doing the work yourself;

— A wall or small room requires a new drywall surface and you will do the work.

II — Some repainting is in order and you will be hiring a contractor to do the job;

— A wall or small room that requires a new drywall surface and you will be hiring a contractor to do it;

— An interior masonry wall needs to be repointed.

III — A substantial area of the house requires all-new surfaces.

Short of an interior where fire or water damage has essentially gutted the walls—and consequently an enormous and expensive reconstruction must be done—there are no Walk-Away Factors at this checkpoint.

WINDOWS AND DOORS

Windows are not to be seen but to be seen through; it should be as if they were not there at all. In fact, windows and doors are usually ignored until problems occur and suddenly one learns to appreciate how important they are.

Windows and doors are crucial to keeping unwanted intruders and the elements outside, and to letting in the breezes and light or visitors when you want them in. As you look at all the windows and doors, your two biggest determinations should be: Are they weathertight? Are they secure? Other concerns are ease of use and appearance.

WINDOWS

Most windows have four basic constituent parts: the frame, sash, glazing, and hardware. The sash contains the glass (or glazing). The movable sash slides or pivots within the frame, while the hardware fasteners or hinges guide or limit that movement.

Windows are of six basic designs: double-hung, sliding, casement, awning, jalousie, and fixed. Double-hung windows are the traditional sliding variety that, within the plane of the wall, travel up and down within their frames. Sliding windows also consist of two sashes that slide within their frames, only rather than sliding up and down they slide side to side.

Casement and awning windows are essentially hinged windows, with one fixed side (a casement window) or the top (an awning window) acting as a pivot for the window to open. Jalousie windows consist of a series of horizontal panes that operate like a louver. Fixed windows do not open, but are glass openings fixed in place.

Open and shut every window in the house: Do all of them work easily, or will they be difficult to open and close for some members of your family? Do the double-hung windows stay open or must they be propped up? If they tend to close by themselves, check for rope and pulley mechanisms in the frames. If you see a pulley inside the frame without a chain or rope linking it to the window, then the weight designed to counterbalance the window is no longer doing its job. It is difficult to correct that problem and requires at least a Handyman's skill with casings and a crowbar to get access to the inside of the frame. Though more difficult to open and shut, generally a double-hung window that has lost its counterweights can still do its job at keeping out the rain and unwanted intruders.

The glass within the frames of each of these designs can be of an almost infinite variety of designs. It may be a single sheet or divided into a number of panes, called lites. Many colonial homes have double-hung windows, with the upper portion of the window, or sash, having six or eight or more panes, with the lower sash usually having the same number. A window of that design is referred to as a "six-over-six" or "eight-over-eight."

Windows also may have layers of glass: double- and

even triple-glazing is common today in new construction because of the increased insulation value it offers but, like a substantial insulation barrier, is rarely found in homes more than ten years old. Such insulating glass involves two or three sheets of glass with a cushion of air hermetically sealed between the panes to act as an insulating barrier to the warmer or cooler exterior temperatures.

Whatever the design of the windows, their purpose is to separate the interior of the house from the climate outside. A well-designed window should keep out both extremes of temperature and humidity from the controlled environment within.

Determine first whether the windows are single- or double- or triple-glazed. This is particularly important in homes that are air-conditioned or heated a significant portion of the year. Given the potential for energy loss through the windows—a double-glazed window has an R-factor of approximately R-3—even a tight, modern, insulated window accounts for significant heating or cooling (and therefore energy) loss.

The glazing of the window can usually be seen by the naked eye, but confirm that it is more than a single thickness by opening the window and pressing a finger onto the outside of a pane and another on the inside: if the glass between is roughly 1/4" thick, the glass is a single thickness; if it is 3/8" or more, it is thermal pane, with that insulating cushion of air between the layers of glass. Another way of determining whether a window is of thermal pane construction (in fact, of defective construction) is the presence of condensation between the layers of glass. It is not possible to remove this condensation so it is necessary to either replace the sash with the defective glass, or to live with it as is. If you opt for the latter alternative, it is unsightly and much less energy-efficient.

Are there storms for each window? A storm can double the R-factor of a single-glazed window by creating an insulating layer of air much as in a double-glazed window. The storm is also important as it reduces the direct infiltration of cold air.

You may wish to purchase storm windows if there are none. For newer homes, stock kits can be purchased for installation by the Apprentice or Handyman. If the house is old, however, you may find that you have to have screens and storms specially made, which will add substantially to the expense. If the house has windows above the first-floor level, the installation is better left to a contractor if you have any doubts about your balance or you do not have adequate and safe ladders.

As important as the glazing is the tightness of the frame: Can you feel a draft coming through? Is the window tight in its frame, or is it loose and rattling? Weather stripping can be added to tighten the window but without it, the loose window is little better than an open window.

Is the frame made of wood or metal? Wood is an excellent insulator, while metal will conduct heat to the outdoors. Metal will also cause moisture to condense on its surface in cold weather; the windows may then develop a layer of frost on them, and, eventually, the metal frame may rust. Consequently, metal frame windows are a distinct liability in colder climes.

Metal sashes are also prone to lose their shape over time and not close well. Sometimes panes will crack, and the hardware will become difficult to move because of rust or the accumulation of layers of paint. In one extreme case we know of in New York's Westchester County, many of the metal casement windows had actually become rusted shut. Given the impossibility of matching the remaining windows and the fact that the windows were only single-glazed, replacement was the only answer. The cost? Nearly twenty thousand dollars for the eight-room house.

Are there any signs of leakage? As the wood around the exterior of the window ages and is subject to the assault of the elements, it may well deteriorate and begin to leak. Is the wood still sound, or are there signs of decay? Don't be fooled by a fresh coat of paint; if the surface is noticeably variegated, it may be the toll taken by the weather.

Inspect carefully around the sash where the glass joins the wood or metal. There should be a weathertight seal between them. Most often this seal is made of glazing compound. It is applied damp as a putty and then hardens. Over the passage of time, particularly if it loses its protective coating of paint, it may crack and deteriorate and need to be replaced. It is not difficult to do (a careful Rookie can learn how to do it with an hour's practice), but it does take time and care, and, in the meantime, its absence will result in a multitude of tiny drafts.

Another issue is whether there is enough light in the room. One rule of thumb is that the window openings should constitute at least 10 percent of the total wall surface. How about the hardware on the window: Will each of them lock tightly or can a burglar easily push one up and make his way in?

In the case of skylights, the considerations are much the same. However, the energy-loss factor is even greater with a skylight, since the warm air in the room will rise up and out at an even greater rate through a skylight.

One other serious problem with skylights is leakage; by their very nature they are more exposed and therefore more subject to leakage. Inspect any skylights extra carefully for water stains and any indications of moisture problems. If you find signs of leakage, the Handyman may want to take on the task of improving the flashing around the skylight.

EXTERIOR DOORS

Interior and exterior doors share one task—closure—but the exterior door must be more than a barrier to sound and sight. Once again, it is weather that must be sealed out, but security is a consideration as well.

As with windows, there are a number of different kinds of doors, but most doors swing open and shut. Swinging doors are generally of two varieties, flush and stile-and-rail doors. Flush doors have a single veneer surface that gives the face of the door a smooth, two-dimensional appearance; the second variety, stile-and-rail doors, are more traditional, constructed of horizontal members (the stiles) linked to verticals (rails), with panels in between.

There are several kinds of sliding doors. Doors that recede into built-in spaces in the walls, called pocket doors, are particularly practical in situations where the door is to be left open most of the time. Another kind of sliding door is the bypass sliding door, where separate doors can be doubled up in front of one another to open one portion of the opening. Folding doors are also useful for some applications.

Exterior doors are usually solid, most often of wood. Metalclad doors, some with a rigid insulation core, are also appropriate for use in fireproof buildings and locations where a high insulation value is desired. Swinging doors are more weathertight than the other designs, although sliding glass doors are increasingly used in exterior applications.

Look first for signs that the doors are not weathertight: Is light visible beneath or at any edge of the door when it is closed? If the temperature is quite different outside, run your hand around the inside of the door frame when it is closed and feel for incoming drafts.

In the case of stile-and-rail doors, look through the closed door for signs of daylight. The shrinkage of wood can lead to minute splits in the panels that will result in heat loss.

Is there a storm door for each swinging door? Is there weather stripping around the door? Check the foot of the door, too: Is the threshold noticeably worn and uneven or decayed? Is cold air allowed to enter there?

With sliding doors, it is particularly important to make sure they work smoothly. Open the doors all the way; if they are not level or if water has been allowed to enter their workings for a prolonged period, they may not work easily. If the sliding doors are glass, which direction do they face? If they face south and there is not sufficient shade, they can overheat a room in the summer; regardless of their facing, they will be a considerable heat drain in cold weather.

Is there a bolt lock on each exterior door for security? Do the knobs and other hardware work easily, or are they worn or rusted or frozen?

INTERIOR DOORS

Most interior doors installed today are hollow-core, but older homes are more likely to have solid doors; hollow-core doors are not as soundproof. Some interior doors have glass panes in them to allow light to pass through when the door is closed, some have louvered panels for ventilation.

If bifold doors are used in closets or other applications, check to make sure they stay on their overhead tracks. Do they stay closed?

If the floor level changes from one room to the next, is there a threshold—a hardwood strip with beveled edges—to prevent tripping those who pass through?

Do the door handles or latches work properly? Are there locks on the bathroom doors? Are there any locks on other doors?

ASSESSMENT OF CHECKPOINT NO. 16

MISCELLANEOUS CONCERNS: Perhaps the most important consideration is energy: Are the doors and windows weathertight? Next is security: Will they keep out intruders? General condition and the need for maintenance are the next criteria: Are you buying a month of Saturdays of labor?

IMMEDIATE IMPROVEMENT INDEX: The following problems demand your attention:

I — Weather stripping needs to be added to loose-fitting windows;

— The windows need to be puttied to cut down on infiltration around the panes;

— The hardware on several windows needs to be replaced or added to foil any burglary attempts;

— An exterior door needs a good bolt lock for security.

II — You need to purchase and install storm windows for energy efficiency;

— Several of the windows are badly deteriorated
and must be replaced, frame, sash, and all;

— You would like one or two new windows or a
new skylight installed;

— A badly deteriorated door needs to be replaced.

III — Many of the windows in the house need to be
replaced.

WALK-AWAY FACTORS: If many of the windows and
doors are badly rusted or broken, they will cost you pre-
cious energy dollars in lost heat. If you feel they must be
replaced, figure that each door or window will cost you a
hundred dollars or more, not including labor. If your budget for improvements does not include this sum—and it
should be roughly doubled for labor—walk away.

THE KITCHEN

To many people the condition of the kitchen and bathrooms is a key determinant in whether or not a house is right for them. The kitchen in particular is a uniquely important space: not only is food prepared and, in many cases, consumed there, but often the kitchen also becomes the principal focus of social activity.

The kitchen is also the most expensive room to remodel, so unless you intend to make a substantial investment in time and money, make sure you are satisfied with what you find at this checkpoint. In the next few pages, we will look as objectively as we can at the kitchen, its layout and appliances, but the first distinctions must be made on subjective grounds. Is it large enough? Is there sufficient light? Do you like the materials used for countertops and cupboard space? How does it compare with the kitchens in the home you live in now or with others you like?

THE LAYOUT

To some degree, what is a desirable kitchen layout is a personal matter, but there are certain guidelines that every kitchen design should obey. First and foremost is the "kitchen-triangle" standard.

The sink, range, and refrigerator should be arranged in a triangular pattern. The perimeter of that triangle should not be more than twenty-two feet; the distance between either of the appliances and/or the sink should not be less than four feet or greater than nine.

If the design of your kitchen defies these geometric rules, the odds are that it is less than the most convenient

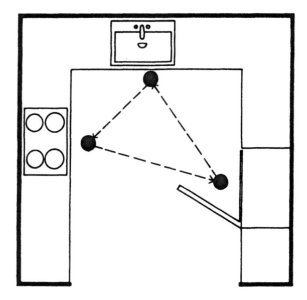

PLATE 5. The Kitchen Triangle

A good kitchen design incorporates a working triangle with the sink, refrigerator, and stove at the three extremities. The total of the sides of the triangle should not be less than 12' but no more than 22'; each side should be between 4' and 9'.

kitchen to use. Walk through the steps you would follow in preparing a simple meal: Are you constantly knocking into the walls of a tiny space? Would a volunteer scullery maid working at your side constantly be in your way as you sautéed your onions? Do you feel like you have to walk a mile to get a splash of cream for your coffee?

Food preparation these days is becoming something of a social activity. If that is true in your household, is the kitchen accessible to social spaces so the cook need not be isolated while cooking?

Is there enough counter space? It is desirable to have counter space on both sides of the sink, that it be at least two feet deep, and that there be a total of at least twenty linear feet. How about cupboard and shelf space? Is there overhead lighting? How about in the vicinity of the cutting board and the stove?

Open the doors to all the appliances. Do they block one another, so that, say, you cannot open the oven door when you're loading the dishwasher? Do any of the doors block the path across the kitchen?

Is there a service exit from the kitchen? Carrying garbage out the front door can be done, of course, but it is preferable to have easy access through another exit to the rubbish storage area. Is there a convenient entrance for bringing groceries in from the car?

THE FLOORS, WALLS, AND CEILINGS

In previous checkpoints we discussed the floor, wall, and ceiling surfaces in the house. In the case of the kitchen, however, the requirements are somewhat different from those of the other rooms.

Chances are water and an endless miscellany of other substances will find their way onto the floor in the kitchen. The walls and ceilings will be subject to a buildup of moisture and heat quite beyond that in the other living areas of the home. Consequently, the materials used should have surfaces that are not easily stained or water-marked.

Inspect the floors, especially in the vicinity of the sink. Are there any water stains apparent? If there are a table and chairs in the kitchen, is the floor noticeably more worn where the chairs slide in and out?

Inspect the wall surfaces beneath the upper cabinets. Pay special attention to the surface behind the stove and sink: those should, respectively, be made of fireproof and waterproof materials.

THE APPLIANCES

Check to see if each appliance works. If one does not, you should negotiate a change in your purchase agreement, and either a new appliance should be installed, or the price adjusted appropriately.

In the case of the stove top or range, make sure all the burners work. Check the oven(s) as well. If the refrigerator or freezer is not in use, turn it on and return the next day to see if it is working properly. If there is no power in the house to run such a check, get the seller to warrant in the contract that the appliances work. In the case of a non-working refrigerator, you should also be sure that the door has not been left tightly closed; if it has, an unpleasant odor may have developed inside, one that is very difficult to get rid of.

Are the seals or gaskets around the refrigerator door tight, or is the plastic worn and torn, which will cause the refrigerators to run inefficiently and expensively? Replacements can be bought and installed by an Apprentice, but for older refrigerators, the parts may be impossible to find.

Is there a vent system for the stove? Does it take the odors and smoke outside, or does it vent them into the attic? The vents that merely filter the smoke then pump it back into the air of the kitchen are less than a satisfactory solution. Installing a new vent system is best left to the Handyman.

In the case of a dishwasher, run it through its entire cycle; you can advance it by hand from one step to the next after it has run for a minute or two in each. Before starting it, however, remove the panel that covers the base (usually it will slide off easily). As the machine runs, take an occasional look beneath the machine to be sure no water is leaking from the tank, pump, or other parts beneath the machine. Do not, however, reach into the nether regions while the machine is running. You should also leave a glass or a coffee cup right side up on the top level of the dishwasher. If no water accumulates in it, the dishwasher pump is not functioning properly.

Run a full cycle with the clothes washer. Check for signs of water at the base and back of the machine. Make sure the clothes dryer warms up and spins properly. Any undue groans or creaks may indicate motor, belt, or bearing problems. If the machine appears of recent vintage, it may be worth having it repaired, but if the machine is clearly of another era, anticipate that the purchase of a new machine will be necessary.

With a garbage disposal, check to be sure it runs properly. If it is one designed with a cap over the drain, is it there and intact? When you run the disposal empty, it should run quietly and smoothly. Loud grinding noises suggest trouble.

Appliance repair is within the province of most well-equipped Handymen. With newer appliances, the Apprentice may feel emboldened to take on some problems, since a number of manufacturers now produce special repair kits complete with parts and instructions written with the nonprofessional in mind.

PLUMBING CONCERNS

Turn the water on in the sink: Does it emerge in a constant, powerful stream or is it merely a trickle? Is the first spurt of water rusty? If so, something in the plumbing is rusted, perhaps the galvanized pipes or the lining of the hot water heater. If the flow is limited, return to Checkpoint 10 and check the pipes. Chances are that they are galvanized and that the insides have accumulated mineral deposits. If, however, the pipes do not appear to be the problem, then the source of water may be the cause. In the next checkpoint we will run a more thorough check on the water pressure.

Do you hear a banging or vibrating sound when you turn the faucets on and off quickly? This is a problem called "water hammering" and it can be cured by installing short, extra lengths of pipe that provide an air cushion to absorb the shock when the flow of water ceases. (Either a plumbing contractor or a Handyman with some plumbing experience can perform this task.) Generally water hammering is little more than an annoyance, though in extreme cases fittings can be loosened over time.

Check the trap under the sink. In Checkpoint 10 we discussed how a U-shaped trap should be located in the drain beneath each plumbing fixture. Be sure that the bottom of the U is located beneath the drain line. If it is not, the trap will not prevent sewer gases from entering the home.

Again, as discussed in the plumbing checkpoint, the drainage system must be properly vented. Otherwise, the traps will have all the water drawn from them. To test this, fill the sink more than half full of water. Open the drain; when the sink is nearly empty, listen carefully. Is there a gurgling or sucking noise as the last of the water disappears? If so, then the vent is not working properly and the trap is being drained. This is a situation that must be corrected.

If there is a sprayer adjacent to the sink, test to make sure it works. Look under the sink to be sure that there is no evidence of any plumbing leaks.

OVERALL CONDITION

Cleanliness is an all-important consideration when it comes to food preparation. You have inspected the appliances and the wall, floor, and ceiling surfaces in the kitchen: Was there a noticeable buildup of dirt and grime anywhere? Were there any signs of an insect infestation? Cockroaches may be the bane of the city cook, but in season the country cook is equally beset by ants. Look out for both.

Check cupboards and closets and the toe space at floor level beneath the cabinets. Is there evidence of frequent, conscientious cleaning? Do the doors on the cupboards and closets open and shut easily or are the latches and hinges in need of repair or replacement? If the home is older, replacing discontinued hardware may be next to impossible. Do they shut tightly? How about drawers?

Are the countertops intact, or are there burns or blemishes? Check beneath appliances or cutting boards or other objects that could be covering such marks. Check the joint between the counter surface and the splashboard: Are there cracks through which water has been seeping? Is the seal around the sink tight, or is there opportunity for leakage there as well?

Are there sufficient electrical outlets? At least one for every three linear feet of counter space is an absolute minimum for most kitchens today.

ASSESSMENT OF CHECKPOINT NO. 17

MISCELLANEOUS CONCERNS: Are there significant plumbing or appliance problems that will require an investment? If not, then think with your heart rather than your head: Can you be comfortable in this all-important room?

IMMEDIATE IMPROVEMENT INDEX: The following problems require correction:

I — There are minor plumbing problems to be fixed, like a leaky faucet or trap;

— Another light fixture is needed;

— The garbage disposal needs repair.

II — A major appliance needs to be replaced;

— A minor remodeling is required involving a new cupboard, a new shelf, or some other limited change in the kitchen;

— The floor needs to be recovered;

— The kitchen counter is badly marred or worn and should be replaced.

III — Two or more major appliances are beyond re-
        pair;

— A substantial remodeling is necessary.

WALK-AWAY FACTORS: In the event a complete remodeling of the kitchen is necessary, make sure you have
the budget for the task. The cost of remodeling can be
limited if you do not need to replace all the appliances and
the talented Apprentice or Handyman takes on some of
the work (note that local building codes may require that
licensed professionals do the electrical and plumbing
work). On the other hand, remodeling a kitchen can be a
very expensive undertaking, costing ten or even tens of
thousands of dollars. If the kitchen needs remodeling and
you simply don't have the money to spend, walk away.

THE BATHROOM

As with the kitchen, a bathroom is a very expensive room to remodel. Remodeling a bath requires more than surface changes, and often involves new fixtures and perhaps even the refurbishing of one of the fundamental working systems in the home, the plumbing.

Usually the problems found in the bathroom of a home are not such that a total renovation is necessary and they are more likely to be a matter of your tastes than of necessity. But if you anticipate a wholesale renovation of one or another of the baths, make sure you have a grasp of the real expense of the project: the price can be many thousands of dollars with expensive tiles or, say, a special-order bathtub, but if you plan to replace even one fixture, the cost will almost certainly exceed a thousand dollars.

One key question to ask yourself is whether the bathroom facilities in the house are sufficient for your needs. If you are accustomed to living in a home with two baths, you may find adjusting to a single bathroom very difficult indeed. A rule of thumb for new construction today is a half bath near the relaxation area and at least one bath for every two bedrooms.

GENERAL CONDITION

Inspect the fixtures. Is the porcelain cracked or broken? Look carefully at the area around the drain in the sink, tub, and shower stall: Are there signs of scarring or pitting? Porcelain fixtures can be re-enameled, but the new finish will not be as durable as the original.

Look particularly closely in and around the shower stall. If the walls are tile, is there any sign of deterioration at the corners or at the point where the shower meets another surface, like a bathtub or shower base? The grout used for the tiles is likely to break down sooner at such points and allow water to escape. If there are cracks or other signs that water is passing through to the wall behind, the fix is much like caulking on the exterior of the house. It involves the same gun and a tube of bathroom caulking (which is more expensive than other varieties, though usually less than ten dollars a tube). A willing Rookie can learn to recaulk quite adequately.

Look for any signs of leakage. Look beneath the sink and the toilet tank. Check the floor for signs of decay, of warping, or other evidence of prolonged exposure to dampness. Some condensation is inevitable, but more than a minor amount can lead to decay in not only the flooring but also the structure of the adjacent floor and walls.

If there are any access doors, open them. Is there evidence of any leakage? Turn on the taps that are fed by the pipes inside the access door: Can you see leaks now? Inspect and check the traps as you did in the kitchen.

Are there shut-off valves for each fixture? Although not essential for normal use, the shutoffs are invaluable for any repair work. Without them the entire system will have to be shut down until the repair is completed. The shutoffs are likely to be beneath the sink and toilet, but in the case of the shower or bath they may be hidden behind an access door in another room or closet. To find them, check the other side of the wall from the fixture; if the bath is on the first floor, the shutoff may be in the cellar below.

Toss a ball of a half dozen or more sheets of toilet paper into the bowl and flush. The water level in the bowl should fall; if it rises first before receding, there is a blockage in the line. In fact, if any of the drains evacuate water excessively slowly (that is, if the faucet is running at a reasonable rate and the sink fills rapidly while the drain is open), you may have a drain problem. A Handyman armed with a tool called a snake (a long, metal cable or wire that bears a certain resemblance to a straightened-out coat hanger) may be able to cure the problem, but if the problem is with the sewage system, it is more serious and should be indicated by the test described in Checkpoint 10. Make sure that you run the test if you found signs of drain trouble here.

WATER PRESSURE

Turn on each of the faucets in the bathroom, as you did in the kitchen. Is the flow strong and even? Check the hot and cold water separately.

Another test you should conduct is to run the water in the sink at full force, then turn on the tap in the tub or shower. Is there more than a slight change in pressure at the sink? Now, flush the toilet and watch the output of the faucets. Some change is normal, but if a torrent lessens to a trickle, the pressure may be a problem. Run this test first with just the hot water, then with the cold.

The cause may be with old galvanized pipes, in which case you may have a substantial repair on your hands (see Checkpoint 10). It may be that the pump in your home is simply overtaxed by the demands put upon it, and short of replacing the pump with one of greater capacity, you may decide to learn to live with the problem.

OTHER CONSIDERATIONS

Is there an electrical outlet to provide current for an electric razor, toothbrush, or hair dryer? Two is better than one, but none should be within reach of the tub or shower. In a recently constructed home, the outlet should be protected by a Ground-Fault Interruptor (GFI), a safety device that functions as a second fuse. In the event of a fault in the ground, it will shut off the power to the outlet, preventing any possibility of electrical shock. You should consider installing GFI outlets if your bathroom does not have them; the Handyman may wish to take this on, though, again, be aware that the local building codes may forbid anyone but a licensed electrician from doing so.

Inspect the traps as you did in the kitchen. Run the half-full sink test, listening for gurgles as the water drains.

Run another test while you're in the bathroom. Wash your hands (the inspection is almost over, anyway). Is it difficult to get the soap to lather? If so, then the water in the house is "hard." This means that the mineral content is high (probably magnesium and calcium in particular) and that those minerals are likely to build up in the pipes and hot water heater. This can shorten their lives, and if you have already noted some plumbing problems (especially galvanized pipe) this may give you pause; it is probably best to assume some plumbing repairs are in your future.

ASSESSMENT OF CHECKPOINT NO. 18

MISCELLANEOUS CONCERNS: Are major renovations necessary? If so, get a licensed plumbing contractor to give you written estimates of the costs.

As usual, consider your tastes and needs. If the house is older and there is no shower stall, check to make sure there is an overhead shower head and that the adjacent walls are tile or some other watertight material. You don't want to move in, get ready for your first shower in your new home, only to discover it isn't possible.

IMMEDIATE IMPROVEMENT INDEX: These problems should be attended to:

I — A faulty trap in a bathroom;

    — Grout in the shower or bathtub that has deteriorated and needs caulking to seal off any leaks;

    — Minor plumbing repairs like a leaky faucet or a toilet that runs constantly.

II — The replacement of a fixture in a bathroom.

III — The installation of a new bath or half bath;

    — A full remodeling of a bathroom.

WALK-AWAY FACTORS: If the bathrooms are simply inadequate to your needs and must be remodeled, make sure your home improvement budget can handle the expense. If not, walk away.

DESIGN AND LAYOUT

You might think that the design and layout of the house is the best place to start the inspection. Our thinking is, however, that it is only after you have looked at all the trees that you can come to some sense of what the forest is really like.

In one of Graham Greene's novels, a character moves from one room to another in an enormous mansion, sleeping only one night in each of the countless bedrooms. If you were to try and do the same, only instead moved to a house of a distinctly different design from one day to the next, you could continue your travels almost indefinitely.

While the purpose of this book is not to provide you with an analysis of the relative merits of every unusual or even commonplace building design, it may be useful for you to distinguish the home you propose to purchase from others in the neighborhood and in your experience.

EXTERIOR APPEARANCES

Residential buildings are of three basic kinds: individual single-family homes; single-family homes that are built in clusters (town house construction, for example); and multifamily apartment or condominium buildings. Portions of this book are applicable only to the single-family home, since some of the exterior and working system checkpoints are outside the concerns and control of the condominium or apartment dweller. In the same way, this checkpoint will also focus on the single-family home.

Individual homes come in a great variety of styles. Colonial styles alone can be divided into at least four different types on the basis of national origin, as English-, Spanish-, Dutch-, and French-influenced designs are distinctively different. The Victorian period offers more variations still, while our century has added its share of innovations with the ranch and split-level and others.

In order to help you understand the house you propose to buy and to relate your interests and problems to it, we will address the basic design distinctions having to do with configurations rather than all of the architectural variations.

THE ONE-STORY HOUSE: The standard ranch is perhaps the best example of the one-story house. It is also the most often-constructed configuration. Its advantages include no stairs to climb and inexpensive construction costs. It is also the easiest to maintain, as there is less climbing of ladders and scaffolding involved with painting and roofing and other tasks.

THE ONE-AND-A-HALF-STORY HOUSE: These days, fewer and fewer one-and-a-half-story houses, a compromise design, are being built. While they do have a second floor, the side walls are not of full height so the upstairs ceilings pitch downward. It is a proven design, however, as the Pilgrims set up housekeeping quite successfully in their one-and-a-half-story Cape Cod designs.

The good news about the one-and-a-half-story arrangement is that a second floor is to be had for next to nothing in terms of building materials and costs. The bad news is that this saving is rarely passed on to the consumer; and to some it doesn't seem like much of a bargain, given the inbuilt limitations on ventilation, light, and headroom on the second floor.

THE TWO-STORY HOUSE: The two-story house is perhaps the classic American family home. Can you imagine any of the television sitcoms of the early sixties without bannisters for the children to slide down on and upstairs bedrooms to banish them to?

It is an efficient design, as, in a sense, it uses one foundation twice and is easy to heat. But there are stairs to climb, a hardship for some.

THE SPLIT-LEVEL: The split-level has compromise written all over it: it draws upon the other designs, in particular the two-story house, but is distinct because its entry is at a level in-between the first and second floors, in a sense "splitting" the house.

The split-level can be constructed on a small lot, as can the two-story house. In doing so, it will take up a minimum of space, while providing a maximum of interior living area.

Areas of the house can be isolated from one another, which can be an advantage. But this design is difficult to heat, and many people find having living areas of the home on the first floor unsatisfactory, because they often feel as if they are underground.

You must weigh the pluses and minuses of the design

of your house; no doubt you bring a number of personal prejudices and tastes to the matter as well. You should also consider whether the house, regardless of its design, is well situated on the property. In very old homes, all too often they are close to the road; when the road was widened to accommodate automobile traffic, the front yard was truncated. Does the house sit at the highest point on the property, offering attractive views of the surrounding area? Does it, in short, take best advantage of the neighborhood and terrain and vegetation?

Another consideration is additions: Is it evident from the style of one portion of the house that it was added later? Many additions add more than space to a house, both good things and bad. A new wing to a home can complement the original, or it can detract from what was there.

One house we inspected on the north shore of Long Island started life as a captain's house at the turn of the eighteenth century. The rooms were small, in keeping with the scale of the people, the heating facilities available at that time, and the lifestyle of pre-Revolutionary Americans. However, its present owner added on a grand room of classical proportions. It has a handsome coffin ceiling, elaborate moldings, and elegant French doors that look out on Long Island Sound. The room is almost palatial. But the house looks like a Model T grafted to a Rolls-Royce.

As you examined your house, did you detect any signs of an addition? If so, does it work with or against the rest of the house? This is a judgment call, but most people can instinctively sense when something is out of balance. Make sure you ask yourself the question.

INTERIOR LAYOUT

You may have a great variety of criteria you wish to apply to the house. If you have a musician in your family, you may require a solid-walled room in an isolated corner of the house that can be used as a music room; if someone who lives with you is confined to a wheelchair, you may be concerned with ramp access to the house and between levels in the home. You know your concerns best; make sure you have them in mind as you think about the house.

Most good designs divide the home into three main areas: the private or bedroom area, the work area (including the kitchen and utility room), and the relaxation area. The latter generally includes the living and dining rooms, sometimes a recreation or family room as well.

Does the layout make allowances for the different uses of the different areas? For example, is the relaxation area immediately below the bedroom area? If so, any entertaining after hours is sure to disturb a nearby sleeper. Is the den or study out of the major traffic lanes?

Measure the rooms. Are they sensibly proportioned to your needs? How about your furniture: Will the giant pier glass from Grandma's house fit into the living room?

Is there a closet in the front hall for coats and a broom closet in the vicinity of the kitchen? How about ample closets in the bedrooms? A linen closet?

Is the overall layout a sensible, workable design?

As with the exterior and any additions, are there signs of substantial renovations? If so, do they work? Here again, common sense and instinct are your best guides. Do things seem right? Are the additions or renovated portions of the house awkward, inconsistent, or jarringly different from the main section? Years ago carpenters worked with plan books and knew how to lay out a house. Many of today's builders have not had specific training in the disciplines of design and planning, and sometimes their work exhibits this inexperience.

MISCELLANEOUS CONCERNS

Another responsibility of a good design and layout is safety. Is there an alternative exit—a second staircase or at least a large window or fire escape—in the event of a fire on the second floor? Each bedroom should have an accessible fire escape route.

Are the stairways sound, or do the treads (the horizontal steps) squeak? A few small noises probably indicate only loose boards; louder, more pronounced groans may suggest more serious problems. Is everything sturdy? Is there evidence of weakness in the carriage, the solid pieces of lumber that support the stairs on each side? Cracks or a noticeable spring to the steps would indicate this kind of trouble. If you suspect it, get a close look at the carriage. Is it sound, or is it separating from its moorings at the head or foot?

Are all of the steps the same height? Sometimes the first or last step is of a different height, increasing the chances of someone tripping. Are any of the treads sagging?

Do all the staircases have handrails? Is there good lighting that provides each step with ample illumination? Can the light be turned on at both the top and bottom of the stairs? Is there sufficient clearance for tall residents or visitors, or will people forever be cracking their heads going up or down? Are the stairs dangerously steep or the treads hazardously narrow?

Are there smoke detectors located on each floor? In particular, is there one in the vicinity of the bedrooms?

Is there a security system? If it was installed by a professional, is the firm still in business to service it? If there is a maintenance contract, how expensive and comprehensive is it?

If the system is store-bought or handmade, does it seem to be functional and well constructed? Frequently one telltale sign of poor installation is that the silver conductor tape on the windows is sloppily applied; another indication are clearly visible wires. Can an intruder disarm the system easily (for example, by cutting the speaker wire running to the external siren)?

Are there basement rooms? Basement rooms whose floor is more than 50 percent below grade (i.e. below ground level) are not legal for sleeping rooms under many building codes.

ASSESSMENT OF CHECKPOINT NO. 19

IMMEDIATE IMPROVEMENT INDEX: These observations demand your attention:

I — The absence of smoke detectors.

II — Stairways in danger of collapse;

— Stairways without guardrails;

— Inadequate fire escape routes from the second floor.

FINAL EVALUATION

We recommend that you come back to this chapter after having completed the inspection. Your final sense of the place is probably best recollected in the tranquility of your present home, in a familiar place with few distractions. There you can absorb what you learned, consider your feelings as well as your thoughts, and try to put them all into perspective.

EXPERT ADVICE: The idea of this book is to provide you with enough of an understanding of the potential problems that you will recognize the big ones when you see them. So if you found any major problems, get a reputable contractor's estimate of the cost and time involved in correcting the problem, particularly if the trouble is in the foundation, the basic structure, or with the working systems. In some cases, the exact diagnosis of the extent and severity of the disease is best left to an expert. This is particularly true when it comes to termites or aluminum wiring, for example.

ROOKIES, APPRENTICES, AND HANDYMEN: When it comes to doing the work yourself, Rookies and Handymen and Apprentices alike should keep in mind that in many states and communities there are limitations on what you are supposed to take on without a license. In many areas, electrical and plumbing work is, by law, the sole province of trained professionals.

You should also make a list of the problems you feel you can take on yourself. All too often the enthusiastic buyer will say to himself, "Oh, that's no big deal, I can fix that." It may be true, but if there are a dozen or more little problems then the sum of them may be a big deal.

Some people find it useful to review the Checksheet carefully and make a separate list of the key trouble points from it. Another list to complement this one is the list of reasons you want the house. Balance the two: Which carries more weight in your eyes?

IMMEDIATE IMPROVEMENT INDEX: You should also separate any entries you made under the heading of the Immediate Improvement Index. Total the *I*-, *II*-, and *III*-rated problems. Multiply the number of entries in each category by $150, $750, and $1,500, respectively. Add the three totals together.

This should be your home improvement budget. It is, of course, wildly approximate (if you have a kitchen remodeling in mind, for example, it may cost you ten thousand dollars and will, obviously, throw this guesstimate of a budget entirely out of balance). Nevertheless, the number you come up with is probably a useful approximation of the minimum expenditure you should allow for correcting the problems listed on the Index.

WALK-AWAY FACTORS: Did you come across any Walk-Away Factors? If so, think long and hard before buying the house in question. As we told you in the Introduction, any problem can be fixed—but for a price. Are you willing to pay it? If you do come across any Walk-Away

Factors, at least take the precaution of getting an expert to examine the problem for you and give you his evaluation of it, along with an estimate of what will have to be done to correct it—and how long it will take and how much it will cost.

TO BUY OR NOT TO BUY: Having walked through the house, covering each of these nineteen checkpoints, you still will have, no doubt, room for worry. We warned you up front—no house is perfect, so you certainly found problems that need to be corrected. But that is not the heart of the matter.

It is easy to say no. There's always tomorrow and another opportunity, but if you do decide to pass on the house, make sure you are doing so for the right reasons. One way to test yourself is to consider whether you would still be interested in buying the house for less money; if so, then perhaps you should try to.

Every situation is different. Only you know what you can (and want) to spend, only the seller knows what he feels he has to get. Use what you learned in your inspection to negotiate as frankly and honestly as possible. And don't be afraid to ask hard questions of the seller; it is you who will have to live there, it is he who has lived there. He knows what you need to know, so ask him. He'll probably be very forthcoming if you can get across to him how sincere and concerned you are.

In thinking about the house, you should allow yourself moments in which you are as subjective as you wish: Will you be proud to show your friends and family around this house?

Somehow, it is only appropriate to bring the inspection to an end on a subjective note. You may live in this house for a number of years; it may become something like a member of your family. Are you going to be thinking of it from day one as the black sheep, unworthy of you and yours?

By this point, you are much better informed than you were at the beginning of the process, but in the end neither volumes of information nor years of education can make the determination for you. If the house is right or wrong for you or your family, you'll know it.

CHECKSHEET

Take the Checksheet (or photocopies of it) with you when you conduct the inspection. The Checksheet is designed to remind you of the crucial concerns raised in the text. Fill in the blanks on the Checksheet during the actual inspection, referring back to the body of the book if questions arise.

PART I. THE EXTERIOR

Checkpoint No. 1
THE YARD AND THE NEIGHBORHOOD

Condition of Lawn and Landscaping: _____Excellent _____In need of minor maintenance _____Requires extensive attention _____Major excavation, planting, and landscaping required

Trees and Shrubs: _____Healthy and well-trimmed _____Minor pruning needed _____Additional planting necessary _____Safety hazard due to overgrowth

Condition of Fences and Other Constructions: _____Excellent _____In need of minor repairs _____Replacement of posts or rails required in one section of fencing _____Major reconstruction required of all or a major portion of the fence

Condition of Driveway and Other Utility Surfaces: _____Excellent _____In need of minor filling at sides _____Requires extensive patching or sealing work _____Major excavation and reconstruction required

IMMEDIATE IMPROVEMENT INDEX:

I _____Decayed fences;
     _____Dead or dangerous branches;
     _____Badly lit front walkway.
II _____Tree to be taken down;
     _____Retaining wall to be built.
III _____Major landscaping job;
     _____Pool or tennis court to be installed.

WALK-AWAY FACTORS:

_____A major polluter in the neighborhood;
_____Location is low-lying area in a damp climate and standing water is evident on the property with no additional drainage available.

Checkpoint No. 2
EXTERNAL WALL COVERINGS

Siding Material: _____Masonry _____Clapboard _____Wood shingles _____Other wood surface _____Aluminum or vinyl siding _____Other_____

Condition: _____Excellent _____Requires painting or other superficial work _____Needs partial replacement _____Must be replaced in total

Decay: _____None _____Dry rot in one confined area _____Widespread decay

Caulking Condition: _____Excellent _____Some recaulking required _____Substantial recaulking needed

IMMEDIATE IMPROVEMENT INDEX:

I _____Efflorescence on brick walls;
     _____Some caulking to be redone;

_____Confined areas of peeling or blistering paint.

II   _____Repointing required on one side of a brick house;

_____A few siding boards or panels need replacement;

_____Much peeling or blistering paint in numerous areas requires repainting;

_____Recaulking required on a great many windows and corners;

_____A few cracks in stucco need patching.

III   _____One or more sides of the house require re-siding;

_____The entire brick house needs repointing;

_____Restuccoing is necessary on one whole side of the house;

_____Entire house needs repainting;

_____There is evidence of some rot in more than one small, confined area.

WALK-AWAY FACTORS:

_____Chronic cracking in a zigzag staircase pattern in masonry walls;

_____Uneven settling evident;

_____Chronic cracking on all sides of a stucco house.

Checkpoint No. 3

INDOOR/OUTDOOR SPACES

Nature of Structure: _____Porch _____Deck

Condition of Flooring: _____Excellent _____Requires painting or other superficial work _____Some softness or decay evident in limited area of floor _____Many floorboards must be replaced

Structural Soundness: _____Excellent _____Indications that decay is under way in limited portion of deck or porch but no structural weakness is evident _____Posts or joists in one section show evidence of decay and require replacement _____Entire support structure must be replaced

IMMEDIATE IMPROVEMENT INDEX:

I   _____A small deck more than a foot off the ground with no guardrail;

_____Deck that needs to be repainted.

II   _____A large deck more than a foot off the ground with no guardrail;

_____Floorboards in a confined part of deck need to be replaced;

_____The posts that support the deck are in contact with the ground and must have concrete footings poured beneath them;

_____Additional support posts must be added.

III   _____Entire deck must be rebuilt;

_____Deck's or porch's supporting structure must be reconstructed.

WALK-AWAY FACTOR:

_____Decay in badly deteriorated porch attached to the house has spread to the main building. Follow up at Checkpoint 6.

Checkpoint No. 4
THE ROOF

Roofing Material: _____Slate or tile _____Wood shingles _____Asphalt shingles _____Flat roof _____Other:

_____

Condition: _____Excellent _____Slight signs of wear _____Replacement necessary of one portion of roof surface _____Entire roof surface must be replaced

Condition of Flashing: _____Excellent _____Signs of previous repairs _____Must be replaced

Chimney Condition: _____Excellent _____Needs some repointing _____Needs flue lining _____Must be rebuilt

Condition of Gutters and Downspouts: _____Excellent _____Need cleaning _____Need some pieces repaired or replaced _____Must be replaced

IMMEDIATE IMPROVEMENT INDEX:

  I _____Minor flashing repairs necessary;
    _____Small repairs are required on the gutters or downspouts.
  II _____Flashing or electrical cables need to be installed to prevent recurrence of ice dams;
    _____Chimney needs repointing or relining;
    _____Gutters and downspouts need considerable repair or replacement;
    _____Chimney needs drip cap;
    _____Major flashing repairs necessary.
  III _____Roof needs to be resurfaced;
    _____Flat roof needs ventilation or runoffs;
    _____Box gutters need reconstruction.

WALK-AWAY FACTOR:

_____Noticeable dips or sags in the roofline indicating structural weakness and roof needs resurfacing. Follow up at Checkpoint 11.

Checkpoint No. 5
THE GARAGE AND OTHER OUTBUILDINGS

Nature of Structure: _____Attached garage _____Separate garage _____Other outbuildings

Condition of Garage: _____Excellent _____Requires painting or other superficial work _____Needs limited carpentry or other attention _____Must be totally reconstructed or replaced

Other Concerns: _____Fire wall missing in attached garage _____Garage door problems

Condition of Outbuilding: _____Excellent _____Usable but
needs work _____Needs major repairs _____Must be torn
down or completely rebuilt

IMMEDIATE IMPROVEMENT INDEX:

    I _____The garage or other outbuilding needs painting.
   II _____The garage needs some minor roof or siding repairs;
         _____The garage door needs replacement;
         _____The garage or outbuilding has no electricity and a
         line must be run from the house.
  III _____The garage needs an entirely new roof surface;
         _____The garage needs to be entirely re-sided;
         _____The garage's foundation shows signs of serious
         decay.

WALK-AWAY FACTORS:

_____You are buying the property expecting that one or several
of the outbuildings will provide you needed space and
they are beyond repair;
_____There are several dilapidated old buildings on the prop-
erty that have to be torn down.

PART II. HIDDEN AND MECHANICAL AREAS

Checkpoint No. 6
THE FOUNDATION

Nature of Foundation: _____Full basement _____Crawl space
_____Slab _____Pier and post

Condition: _____Excellent _____Efflorescence or deteriorating
mortar _____Serious signs of shifting and cracking

Dampness and Decay: _____None _____Moisture but no noticeable decay _____Definite dry rot in structural members

IMMEDIATE IMPROVEMENT INDEX:

I _____There is no vapor barrier in the crawl space.

II _____The ventilation in the basement or crawl space is inadequate;

_____The basement is chronically damp but there is no accompanying decay in the wood structure of the house;

_____The lower ends of wooden posts in a pier-and-post foundation are immersed in concrete footings;

_____The chimney foundation is evidently weak.

III _____There is decay in a confined area of the cellar;

_____One wall or a small section has decayed.

WALK-AWAY FACTORS:

_____Numerous cracks or other signs of uneven settling;

_____Seriously decayed support members to the house.

Checkpoint No. 7

TERMITES AND OTHER INSECTS

Insect Infestation: _____None _____Subterranean termites (key indication: shelter tubes) _____Dry-wood termites (small pellets) _____Carpenter ants (sawdust) _____Powder-post beetles (exit holes)

IMMEDIATE IMPROVEMENT INDEX:

I _____A minor infestation of insects.

II _____A more serious infestation in which one discrete portion of the house has been damaged and some carpentry and other work is required.

III _____A major, long-term assault by termites or other insects.

WALK-AWAY FACTOR:

_____An insect infestation that has been present for many
years.

Checkpoint No. 8
THE ELECTRICAL SYSTEM

Service Entrance: _____200 amps _____150 amps _____100
amps _____60 or less amps

Fuse Box or Breaker Panel: _____Fuses _____Circuit breakers
   Number of 15-amp circuits _____
   Number of 20-amp circuits _____
   Other _____

Wire Insulation: _____Cloth _____Plastic

Plug Receptacles: _____Three-pronged _____Two-pronged

IMMEDIATE IMPROVEMENT INDEX:

   I _____The service drop has worn insulation or branches
         interfere with it;
      _____There is dampness or standing water in the imme-
         diate area of the electrical panel;
      _____There is not a proper ground for the electrical sys-
         tem;
      _____One or two outlets or light fixtures need to be fixed
         or replaced.
   II _____There is unsafe fusing in the panel;
      _____Outmoded wiring in the house will have to be re-
         placed.
   III _____The size of the service entrance must be increased.

WALK-AWAY FACTOR:

_____The house has been inadequately, carelessly, and danger-
ously wired.

Checkpoint No. 9
HEATING AND AIR-CONDITIONING

Nature of Boiler System: _____Gravity hot water _____Forced hot water (key indication: circulating pump) _____Steam (single-pipe radiators)

Nature of Furnace System: _____Gravity hot air (key indication: vent in side of furnace) _____Forced hot air

Fuel: _____Gas _____Oil _____Electricity _____Other:
_____

Indications of Exhaust Leakage: _____Yes _____No

Indications of Boiler Leakage: _____Yes _____No

Electric Baseboard Heat: _____Yes

Area Heaters: _____Yes   Kind: _____

Air-Conditioning System Test: _____No problems indicated _____Frequent starting and stopping _____Refused to run

IMMEDIATE IMPROVEMENT INDEX:

I _____Walls or ceilings of flammable materials must be protected by gypsum board or other fireproof material;
_____There is insufficient ventilation in the burner area;
_____There is no pressure-relief valve on the steam or hot water system;
_____There are no pressure or temperature gauges on the steam or hot water system;
_____There is no emergency shutoff for the furnace or boiler.
II _____Pipes are rusted or corroded;
_____The oil storage tank must be replaced;
_____A new firebox or boiler tank is necessary;
_____Substantial maintenance is necessary on the central air-conditioning system.
III _____The boiler or furnace must be replaced.

WALK-AWAY FACTOR:

_____The entire heating system needs to be replaced or radically overhauled.

Checkpoint No. 10
WATER, PLUMBING, AND HOT WATER HEATERS

Source of Water: _____Municipal _____Shallow well
_____Deep well

Shut-off Valves: _____Main _____For each fixture

Hot Water Heater: _____Independent _____Attached to heating system burner

Hot Water Output Calculation: _____Adequate _____Marginal _____Insufficient

Pipes: _____Copper _____Galvanized _____Brass _____Plastic

Condition of Pipes: _____Excellent _____No leakage at present, but water stains present _____Leaking

Drainage and Sewage Problems: _____Improper traps _____Inadequate pitch on drainage pipes _____Slow flow from drains

IMMEDIATE IMPROVEMENT INDEX:

I _____The gas or hot water heater vent pipe allows fumes or smoke to enter the house;
_____No pressure and temperature release valve on the hot water heater;
_____The flame on the hot water heater needs adjustment;
_____A limited number of repairs are needed on the pipes in the plumbing system;
_____Several fixtures have no or improper traps.
II _____The pump in the well must be replaced;
_____The storage tank must be replaced;

_____The hot water heater must be replaced or over-hauled;

_____A number of pipes will need to be replaced;

_____The vent pipe ends must be extended through the roof.

III _____A new well must be dug;

_____The sewage system must be radically improved or replaced.

WALK-AWAY FACTORS:

_____The entire house must be replumbed;

_____No source of clean water available.

Checkpoint No. 11
THE ATTIC

Nature of Attic: _____Finished _____Full unfinished _____Crawl

Dampness and Decay: _____None _____Moisture but not noticeable decay _____Decay in structural members

Ventilation: _____Adequate _____Marginal _____Insufficient

Miscellaneous Concerns: _____Attic fan _____Chimney requires repair

IMMEDIATE IMPROVEMENT INDEX:

I _____There are no fire-stops around the entrance of the chimney or furnace vent pipe at the attic floor.

II _____Vents or louvers must be installed in the attic;

_____Some roof work must be done (See Checkpoint 4);

_____Chimney work must be done.

III _____Considerable roof work must be done.

WALK-AWAY FACTOR:

_____The roof has an evident bow in it, especially if the house is relatively new.

Checkpoint No. 12
INSULATION

Ceiling Insulation: Kind: _____
    Quantity: _____Adequate _____Insufficient

Wall Insulation: Kind: _____
    Quantity: _____Adequate _____Insufficient

Vapor barrier: _____In floor _____In ceiling _____In walls
_____Can't tell

IMMEDIATE IMPROVEMENT INDEX:

   I _____There is no insulation around the duct work of the
           central air-conditioning system.
  II _____There is no insulation in the unfinished or crawl
           attic of the house.
 III _____There is no insulation in the walls of the home.

PART III. THE LIVING AREAS

Checkpoint No. 13
FIREPLACES AND CHIMNEYS

Condition of Fireplace: _____Excellent _____In need of cleaning _____Requires repointing _____Substantial reconstruction
required

Damper: _____Yes _____No   Flue lining: _____Yes
_____No

IMMEDIATE IMPROVEMENT INDEX:

   I _____The chimney must be cleaned.
  II _____Two or more chimneys need to be cleaned;
           _____A chimney must be repointed or lined.
 III _____More than one chimney must be lined;
           _____A chimney has a foundation that has settled un-
           evenly and requires substantial reconstruction.

WALK-AWAY FACTOR:

_____The principal source of heat for the home utilizes an unsafe chimney.

Checkpoint No. 14

FLOORS

Flooring Material: _____Hardwood _____Softwood
_____Tile _____Flexible flooring _____Wall-to-wall carpeting

Condition: _____Excellent _____Requires refinishing
_____Signs of curling or cupping or shrinkage, and needs considerable work _____Floor surface must be replaced

Structure: _____Sound _____Some sign of shifting or squeaking floorboards _____Floor spongy and badly deteriorated

IMMEDIATE IMPROVEMENT INDEX:

I _____Flexible flooring must be replaced in one room.
II _____Wood floors must be sanded and refinished;
_____Many tiles are cracked and broken in a tile floor.
III _____A wood or tile floor must be taken up and replaced.

Checkpoint No. 15

INTERIOR WALLS AND CEILINGS

Material: _____Gypsum board _____Paneling _____Masonry
_____Other: _____

Condition: _____Excellent _____Require refinishing
_____Signs of deterioration, need considerable attention
_____Must be replaced

Moldings and Trim: _____All in place and in good repair
_____Some pieces missing or in need of painting _____Considerable work required

IMMEDIATE IMPROVEMENT INDEX:

I _____You will be repainting one or two average-sized
rooms;

_____A wall or small room requires a new drywall sur-
face and you will do the work.

II _____A contractor will be doing some repainting;

_____A wall or small room requires a new drywall sur-
face and will be fixed by a contractor;

_____An interior masonry wall needs to be repointed.

III _____A substantial area of the house requires new surfaces.

Checkpoint No. 16
WINDOWS AND DOORS

Nature of Windows: _____Double-hung _____Sliding
_____Casement _____Awning _____Jalousie _____Fixed

Glazing: _____Single-pane _____Double-glazed _____Triple-
glazed

Storm Windows: _____Yes _____No   Tight fit in frames:
_____Yes _____No

Nature of Doors: _____Flush _____Stile-and-rail

Exterior Door Material: _____Wood _____Metalclad
_____Glass

Security: _____Bolt locks on all exterior doors _____Some
_____None

IMMEDIATE IMPROVEMENT INDEX:

I _____Weather stripping needs to be added to loose-fitting
windows;

_____The windows need to be reputtied;

_____The hardware on several windows needs to be re-
placed or improved;

_____An exterior door needs a good bolt lock for security.

II _____You need to purchase and install storm windows for energy efficiency;

_____Several windows must be replaced;

_____You would like one or two new windows or a new skylight installed;

_____A badly deteriorated door needs to be replaced.

III _____Many windows in the house need to be replaced.

Checkpoint No. 17
THE KITCHEN

Kitchen Triangle: _____Within specifications _____Too small _____Too large

Counter Space: _____Sufficient _____Too little

Floor: _____Waterproof surface in good condition _____Needs repair _____Must be replaced

Range Condition: _____Excellent _____In need of cleaning but functional _____Not working

Refrigerator Condition: _____Excellent _____In need of cleaning but functional _____Not working

Dishwasher Condition: _____Excellent _____In need of cleaning but functional _____Not working

Miscellaneous Concerns: _____Garbage disposal not working _____No hood vent over stove _____Water pressure insufficient _____Too few electrical outlets

IMMEDIATE IMPROVEMENT INDEX:

I _____There are minor plumbing problems to be fixed, like a leaky faucet or trap;

_____Another light fixture is needed;

_____The garbage disposal needs repair.

II _____A major appliance needs to be replaced;

_____A minor kitchen remodeling is required;
_____The floor needs to be recovered;
_____The kitchen counter must be replaced.
III _____Two or more major appliances require replacement;
_____A substantial remodeling is necessary.

WALK-AWAY FACTOR:

_____If the kitchen must be remodeled and you simply don't have the money to spend, walk away.

Checkpoint No. 18

THE BATHROOM

Number of Baths: _____One _____One and one half _____Two _____Two and one half _____Three or more

Plumbing Condition: _____Excellent _____No leakage now, but water stains present _____Leaking

Water Pressure Test: _____Ample pressure _____Some decrease when three or more faucets running _____Significant decrease when second faucet turned on

Miscellaneous Concerns: _____No shut-off valves for each fixture _____No electrical outlets _____Improper traps _____Hard water (indication: soap difficult to lather)

IMMEDIATE IMPROVEMENT INDEX:

I _____A faulty trap in a bathroom;
_____The shower or bathtub needs caulking;
_____Minor plumbing repairs are required.
II _____A fixture in a bathroom must be replaced.
III _____A new bath or half bath must be installed;
_____A full remodeling of a bathroom is required.

WALK-AWAY FACTOR:

_____If the bathrooms are simply inadequate for your needs and your home improvement budget cannot handle the expense, walk away.

Checkpoint No. 19
DESIGN AND LAYOUT

House Configuration: _____One-story _____One-and-one-half-story _____Two-story _____Split-level Other: _____

Layout: _____Bedroom close to entertaining areas _____House separated into three reasonably distinct areas

Fire Escape Routes from All Bedrooms: _____Yes _____No

Stairways Safe: _____Yes _____No

IMMEDIATE IMPROVEMENT INDEX:

I _____Smoke detectors must be installed.
II _____A stairway is in danger of collapse and needs to be reconstructed;
_____There are stairways without railings;
_____Inadequate fire escape routes from the second floor are insufficient.

GLOSSARY

Awning window: A window that hinges at the top and swings outward

Batt or blanket insulation: Insulation that is often fiberglass; available in various widths (12″ to 24″) and lengths (48″ and up) and thicknesses (3″ to 9″); with the consistency of sponge cake

Beam: Main horizontal structural member in the construction of a frame house (see Post, Joist, and Stud)

Brick veneer: A facing of brick laid against and fastened to a frame wall; the masonry is not structural in a veneer wall

Bridging: Supporting technique of placing either solid member ("solid bridging") or pairs of smaller dimension wood pieces in an X pattern ("cross bridging") between adjacent joists to prevent twisting

British thermal unit (BTU): A unit of measure of heat; one BTU is the quantity of heat needed to raise the temperature of one pound of water one degree Fahrenheit

Casement window: A window that hinges at the side and swings outward

Casing (window and door): The molding used to trim door and window openings at the jambs

Caulk: Sealant used to close joints between two materials to make them watertight

Chair rail: An interior molding located at waist height that is intended to protect wall surfaces

Checking: Fissures that appear in wood with age and weathering that, though at first only superficial, eventually may penetrate deeply through the finish

Circuit breakers: Electrical switches that automatically cut off the current in a line when an overload occurs; used instead of fuses in most new construction

Cornice: The decorative horizontal finish that projects at the crown of an exterior or interior wall

Curb valve: The shut-off valve in a home supplied with municipal water

Double-hung window: A window that slides up and down within its frame

Drywall: *See* Gypsum board

Eave: The portion of the roof that, at its lowest edge, projects beyond the building wall

Efflorescence: On masonry surfaces, the white powdery substances brought to the surface by water or moisture; composed of soluble salts

Electrical panel: The box in which the fuses or circuit breakers are located

Firebox: The portion of a fireplace or furnace where the fire or flame is located

Fire-stop: Horizontal wood strips between structural members that limit the spread of fire (also called "blocking" and "fire blocking")

Fixture risers: The vertical plumbing pipes that carry the water, hot or cold, to each fixture

Flashing: Sheet metal (most often copper or aluminum) or other material used in roof and wall construction to protect the joints in a building from being penetrated by water

Footing: Concrete, usually rectangular in shape, set below grade level, onto which the foundation wall or piers are set; the footing distributes the weight of the building onto undisturbed earth around the foundation

Frame construction: Construction in which the structural parts are wood or depend upon a wood frame for support (as in a brick veneer wall)

Frost line: The depth the frost penetrates into the earth in a given location

Gable: The end wall of a building formed by the eave line of a double-sloped roof

Galleries: The tunnels that termites eat on the inside of a piece of wood

Gypsum board: Finish material for walls or ceilings that consists of a layer of gypsum sandwiched between two layers of paper; also called drywall because it is applied dry (unlike plaster whose finish it resembles)

Jalousie window: A window that is made up of a series of horizontal panes that hinge; the entire mechanism functions as an adjustable louver to control ventilation

Jamb: The side or head lining of a door, window, or other opening

Joist: One of a series of parallel beams, usually of lumber of nominal two-inch thickness, that support floor or ceiling loads; joists are, in turn, supported by large beams or bearing walls

Lag bolt: Heavy wood screw

Lath: In wet-wall construction (i.e. when the plaster is applied wet rather than in dry gypsum boards), the lath is the wood, metal, or other material that is attached to the frame of the building prior to plastering to act as a base for the plaster

Lintel: A horizontal member that supports the load over an opening, such as a door, window, or fireplace

Lites: Individual panes of glass within a window sash

Masonry: Brick, concrete, stone, or other similar building units or other materials bonded together with mortar to form walls, piers, buttresses, or other masses

Meter pad: The electrical box into which the utility company's meter is plugged

Picture molding: Interior molding located immediately below the ceiling that is used for attaching hooks for hanging picture frames

Pier: A masonry column used to support the structure of the house

Plenum: The chamber immediately above the furnace that distributes the hot air to the various ducts

Pointing: The filling of open mortar joints between masonry units (brick, stone, block); when over time the mortar has deteriorated and has to be replaced, the term is "repointing"

Polyvinyl chloride (PVC): A type of plastic pipe most often used for drainage, though some building codes will allow it to be used for delivery of the water as well; also called CPVC

Post: Main vertical structural member in the construction of a frame house *(see* Beam, Joist, and Stud)

Rafter: One of a series of inclined structural members that support the roof, running from the exterior wall to the ridge beam or board

Repointing: *See* Pointing

R-Factor: Measurement of insulating ability; the higher the R-Factor, the greater the insulating value. Also referred to as R-Value.

Riser: The vertical board that closes the space between the treads of a stairway *(see also* Tread and Stringer)

Sash: The single, light frame that holds the glass in a window unit

Sheetrock: *See* Gypsum board

Shelter tube: Mud tunnel built by termites between the ground and the wood structure of a house

Sill: The lowest member of the wood framing of a house, the sill rests on top of the foundation wall

Soffit: The underside of an overhanging cornice

Stair carriage: *See* Stringer

Stringer: The sides of the staircase onto which the risers and treads are affixed; also called stair carriage

Stud: One of a series of vertical wood or metal structural members, usually (in the case of wood) of nominal two-inch thickness, used as supporting elements in walls or partitions

Trap: The U-shaped piece of pipe found beneath all plumbing fixtures; gravity holds a small amount of water at its base which prevents sewer gases from entering the home

Tread: The horizontal board on a staircase; colloquially called the step *(see* Riser and Stringer)

Weather stripping: Sections of metal, plastic, felt, or other material used to line the sides, top, or foot of doors or windows to prevent infiltration of air and moisture

Weep hole: The opening at the base of a retaining or masonry veneer wall that allows water to drain

INDEX

CPSIA information can be obtained at www.ICGtesting.com
Printed in the USA
LVOW10s2209190715

446843LV00001B/24/P